Successful Solicitor:

Get ahead of the game as a
junior corporate lawyer

Katherine Cousins

Published in the United Kingdom by Buggle Publishing
Lytchett House, 13 Freeland Park, Wareham Road, Lytchett
Matravers, Poole, Dorset, BH16 6FA
www.successfulsolicitor.co.uk

ISBN: 1-9996395-0-2
ISBN-13: 978-1999639501

Cover design by Book Beaver

DEDICATION

To Greg, for believing in me long, long before I believed in myself. It was always you.

CONTENTS

ACKNOWLEDGMENTS

I have so many people to thank for their patience and generosity in helping me get this book to completion. Thank you to Will Barber, a best friend and in this case careful editor. Thank you for making me sound far less annoying than I do in real life! To the lawyers, Brad Pawlak, Benedict West, Lucie Fortune, Dragana Cvejic, Helen Raynsford-Park, Peetra Anderson-Figeroa, Beatrice Cameli, James Fairburn and Andrew Lister, thank you for your wise insights, your proof-reading skills, and for general cheerleading and professional support. It really has meant the world to me. Steve Weiner, for making me just go for it on more occasions than you knew! Mum, thank you for reading cover to cover and always expecting the best of me. My brother, Richard, for lending his art and design talents. And to Greg, the love of my life and the best coach, partner and friend I could ever ask for. Thank you for endlessly and selflessly supporting all my crazy endeavours. I wouldn't want to do it without you.

OPENING REMARKS: WHO AM I AND TO WHOM AM I WRITING?

Hi! I am Katherine and I'm writing to YOU, the bright, excited young lawyer at the start of your career, who wants honest, actionable advice from someone who's been there not so very long ago. I wrote this book for you, because in effect I wrote it for myself of three years ago. Past Katy would have LOVED to read this book. Back then I looked around for advice on how to make a good first impression, how do my job better, for information on all the little things I felt I didn't understand. And I quickly got tired of the generic, outdated and just plain bland advice out there. Everyone was saying the 'right' thing and no one was saying the 'real' one. It's like there's a script we're all supposed to follow and, even though everyone knows it's a lie, we self-police in case the mythical partner overlords hear us complain about working another weekend and we are barred by the SRA forever. Or… something… I don't know exactly. I just know that I did it too. And it doesn't help anyone.

This is not another dry prescription on 'how to

get a training contract'. There are enough of those in the world. As part of my research I checked a few of them out. This is one of the suggestions I found for how to prepare for an interview:

"The interview process at many firms is based on a combination of them getting to know you and you getting to know them. Firms expect you to have solid reasoning for your choice to enter the legal profession and this commonly means having an interest in a certain type of law. However firms are also aware that trainees learn a lot over the course of a TC and therefore we shouldn't be too closed minded."

Gads! I'm both bored AND I have no idea how to apply that to myself! It's just meaningless corporate, graduate recruitment speak, parroted off like wisdom.

Worse, when I googled 'How to be a great junior solicitor' almost everything that came up was from BigLaw, America. And, well, they do things differently there. For instance, let's not take advice from this guy:

"Only after you've rammed your head against the wall until it's bloody should you come ask a question. I want to know that you've tried to figure it out on your first try (i.e., don't waste my time, it's much more valuable than yours)."

Because he is both rude and quite, quite wrong.

So I wrote this for you. You who feels as though there was an instruction manual handed out somewhere along the way and you must have just missed getting in that line at the library. I know you're out there, because I know that's how I felt. We're so used to getting 'A's and doing whatever we do to the best of our considerable abilities, that it feels awful to be trying your hardest and still missing a trick. My friends and fellow trainees seemed to 'get it' and I just couldn't figure out what I was doing wrong. As it turned out, it was probably nothing, but there was still a lot more I could have been doing right. So for you guys, **this** is that manual.

This book has all the tips, tricks, hacks and lessons I've learned in my past five years as a trainee and now associate. It's all the wisdom imparted during mentoring meetings and appraisals, the suggestions from my super-successful solicitor contemporaries and the lessons I've learned the hard way (read: by messing things up and having to fix them). I trained at a top ten London City firm, qualified into a top 5 global firm and now work at a boutique, specialist US practice. All high-calibre places to be, surrounded by lawyers at the top of their fields. I know my stuff. But I'm not a natural at this like some people. I've had to work really hard to figure out how to succeed and play the game in a way that works for me. And now I want to help you find the way that works for you.

Now let's get some things on the table: I have cried in the toilets on multiple occasions. I've gotten far too drunk at graduate recruitment events. I've left my phone off for **days** when on holiday and I've read the FT for two hours and listed it as 'business development research' on my timesheets. I've also worked 80-hour weeks, finished urgent tasks from the Eurostar/my hotel room/the start line of a marathon. I've managed global compliance projects and been a part of multiple headline grabbing cases and mergers. The first batch is as real and true as the second. I'm human. And I'm an excellent lawyer. But I haven't always felt like it.

If you have felt, like I did, that you don't quite 'get it', but you really want to, this is for you. If you're doing ok, but you want to know how to be brilliant, then read on. If you're great at the technical side, but keep being told you need to work on your interpersonal skills, come on in. Those guys who seem to have been born for this, who never have a moment of self-doubt, or feel the sting of fluffing something up, this is not for them. They've already got enough. This is for you, my fellow human lawyer. There's room for us in here too. Let's go be outstanding, shall we?

Katherine

SECTION 1: GETTING IN THE DOOR, GETTING THE BASICS UNDER YOUR BELT

Step one to becoming a great commercial lawyer is securing a job at a great commercial firm, so we start here with the interview process and a step-by-step guide to anxiety-free (or greatly reduced) interviews. Then, once you're through the door, we look at ways to make an excellent first impression on your new co-workers and how to use questions to get stuck in on your new cases and matters. Lastly in this section, we look at some of the biggest mistakes trainees and NQ's make, ways to avoid them, and some low-hanging fruit you can pick that will make you stand out from your peers as particularly promising.

HOW TO KILL IT AT INTERVIEW

I used to absolutely hate interviews, especially the group assessment centre kind, like those you must endure for vac schemes and training contracts. That kind of competitive hothouse was never my gig. I could front it out, but underneath they made me want to run and hide beneath the nearest available desk. I didn't like the person I had to pretend to be in order to succeed in that environment. It really seems to suit the kind of extrovert blowhards who never seem unsure of themselves even for a second. Thankfully, these types of interviews disappear once you're in a law firm and allowed to be a real person, not just 'potential trainee number 5'.

This chapter assumes that you are past that stage. There is a lot of information out there already, from articles on lawcareers.net to kindle books on Amazon, written by experts on the subject of application forms and assessment centres. Truth be told I completed only one full application process (and got the job. Yay!), so I don't consider myself well versed on the subject. I defer to the aforementioned expert sources if that is what you need right now.[1] Here we focus on the one-to-one, or more than often the two or three-to-

---

[1] https://www.lawcareers.net;
https://www.legalcheek.com/legal-cheek-careers

one, style of interview that either completes a vacation scheme/training contract application cycle or comprises the whole of it in the case of NQ positions and beyond. With these you often have very little inkling of what might be asked or the type of structure the meeting might take. So, first things first:

1. Get the lowdown

Ask your recruiter (assuming you're using one, and you should) for any background they have on the firm or the partners interviewing you. Have they had any candidates interview with this firm in the past? What were they asked? Does the recruiter know what the partners are looking for? This will allow you to tailor your responses to show you meet their needs.

Use LinkedIn and the firm's website to find out about the people interviewing you. What are they known for? What big cases or transactions have they worked on recently? Bonus points if you've worked on anything similar. Bring that up if you can. Check the legal news sites for any recent stories on the firm or the partners. Learn the name of the managing partner and the firm's main advertising line – how do they want to be seen? Chambers and Roll on Friday both have excellent and honest firm profiles on their sites.

2. Prepare, prepare, prepare

You may not know the exact questions or format, but the chances are that you will encounter some variation of the following questions in your interview. I set them out here with some pointers from my own responses as my career coach[2] taught me. The key thing is that you're creating a narrative, telling them a story about you and why you are the best candidate for this role.

a. So, tell us about yourself

This is the **worst** if you've failed to prepare! It's so open ended you'll find yourself starting with how you learned to swim on a family holiday in Cornwall aged four and finish up five minutes later waffling about how your favourite food is a chicken burrito. You may think you can make it up on the fly, but nerves kick in and you'll have no idea what you just said till it comes back to haunt you on the train home: "Why was I talking about that 10k I ran in 2012?!"

Fully prepared, this is your chance to create a cohesive and compelling 'story of you'. Remember this is an interview not a social engagement, so focus on your school, university and work. How do they all fit together? I can draw a clear line from my Dad working for NATO when I was a child, to my love of politics, studying international relations and working in EU law. Think about how your choices fit together – what's the thread connecting them all?

b. Why should we choose you?

Again, so hard to answer off the cuff. Most of us

---

[2] The very excellent David Black:
https://www.linkedin.com/in/davidblack1/

are naturally averse to blowing our own trumpet and that's what you're being asked to do here. That said, remember that the focus of the question is not, 'why are you so good?', but 'why would you be so good for **us**?'. Think about the qualities you have that make you a great employee and a great lawyer (albeit a baby one). Remember that you could be the most technically able person in the world but if you're a total asshole people won't want to work with you.[3]

Pick three qualities you feel make you a good candidate and back them up with real examples. For instance, one of my responses is that I am tenacious. I give the example of working on my Masters in Education while teaching full time, how it was incredibly tough and how I often felt out of my depth. But I kept reading and working and trying until one day it started to make sense. I didn't give up, no matter how much I struggled. I then link this to how, as a junior lawyer, we are often asked to do things well out of our comfort zone or about which we feel unsure. I can take what I learned during my teaching and apply it to my new career as a lawyer.

c. Why do you want to work here?

This should be a mixture of candidly describing how the firm fits your personality and work style with a little bit of flattery thrown in. In my last

---

[3] Obviously, there are some complete psychopaths in law firms, but I think they're tolerated less well now than they might have been a decade ago. Being personable and winning clients over is so important to the bottom line.

interview for a top 5 global firm, I talked about the quality of the work and the opportunity for me to stretch and grow, as they were a rapidly expanding team. This is where you apply what you have learned in your research on the firm.

Other questions/topics you may want to prepare for include:

    i.   Why law?

    ii.   Why are you leaving your existing firm? – Stay positive! Under no circumstances badmouth your current employer. It's petty and never sounds good. Here is most definitely the place for some white lying.

    iii.   Your main successes in your previous role – think best client relationships, biggest projects etc.

    iv.   Your biggest mistake – choose something you ultimately overcame, or better, improved upon for next time.

    v.   Your worst quality – hint: don't say you're a perfectionist. Yawn. And totally transparent. Try to think of something everyone can relate to (procrastinating over difficult tasks, for example) and explain how you work to mitigate it.

3. Practice, practice, practice

Now you have your answers, practice them. Like a Sim earning their charisma points, stand in front of your mirror and read them aloud. Then put your notes down and try again. I boiled my long-form answers down to bullet points, then keywords, and practiced till I just needed to remember my keyword prompts. You can have notes in most interviews, but it looks much better to just have a page of speaking prompts to remind you of your best points. You don't want to be eyes down and reading off the page the whole time. Keep it natural. You only need to hit your big marks. It'll sound weird if you're monologuing away, like you're auditioning for the school play.

4. Tell the truth, but not the whole truth

Everyone knows not to lie at interview, but it is like dating or advertising. You need to be honest, but you can, and should, hold some things back. For instance, tell the story about how you overcame a series of massive setbacks to get the deal closed on time. Do not add that you cried in the toilet every day for a week before it was fixed. Show your good side to the camera.

5. You get to ask questions too!

One of the best things you can do to seal the deal is ask intelligent questions. A great finishing question I have often used is one that came from my teaching background – what would success look like? Ask: *If I am successful in getting this role, what would success look like for me in a year's time?* This has two benefits. Firstly, you're planting the idea that you will get the job in your interviewer's minds and secondly, you're finding out what they want from their junior lawyers. Even if you don't get this job, that's useful information to have going forwards.

Some standard questions are things like: Where does the work come from? Is it funnelled from other parts of the firm or does the team self-generate? What is the structure of the team? What is the training like? And so on.

A final excellent piece of advice given to me by a friend and colleague is: Ask the partners about themselves - Why did you join the firm? Why have you stayed? What is the most interesting matter you've worked on? People like talking about themselves. Often, they are (in most cases very rightly) proud of their work and their firm and love having an audience to share that with. Plus, it leaves a good feeling with them once you leave. They'll feel like it went really well even if they can't put their finger on quite what it was that you said or did to make them feel that way.

6. Technical questions: It's ok if you don't know the answer

It is ok if you don't know the answer to a technical question. This used to scare the hell out of me, like an exam you couldn't revise for because the syllabus is **everything about your subject ever**. But having successfully gotten job offers for interviews where I had to admit I couldn't answer the question, I can honestly tell you it's not about giving the right answer. It's about seeing how you think and how you react to not knowing what to say.

Don't try to fudge an answer. You'll sound like an idiot. Lawyers should be comfortable saying, "I don't know". An NQ who thinks they know everything, or that they can blag it, is a total liability. Ask them to explain it to you. At one of my best interviews, I admitted I didn't know how to approach the question. The partner explained the tricky concept to me and then helped me work through a problem applying it. Even if I hadn't gone on to get the job, I'd have learned something valuable for next time.

There is a caveat to this. You can't know everything, but you should know some things. This will of course depend on your area of law, but if I as a competition lawyer didn't know the definition of Article 101(1) TFEU, that would probably be a problem...

7. Follow up

Send a brief 'thank you for your time' email to the partner(s) who interviewed you, preferably the day after your meeting. Nothing more than that. You can follow up on any outstanding points or share an article you spoke about, but don't force it if nothing obvious springs to mind. A simple thank you will suffice. But DEAR GOD do NOT make a spelling mistake in this email. God. Shudder.

Lastly, remember interviews are a bit like dating. It's a two-way process. You have to like them, too. It doesn't look great to hop jobs too often, so even if you're ecstatic to have been made an offer, take a second to gut check whether this is somewhere you can see yourself for two years or more. Are they people you want to work with? You can ask to meet the rest of the team before you commit. And you can almost always negotiate wages and start date. Remember, you're a valuable asset and they'd be lucky to have you. This absolutely goes for dating, too.

BONUS ROUND: MY INTERVIEW QUESTION MODEL RESPONSES FOR A NEWLY QUALIFIED ROLE

1. Why did you choose to train with [training contract firm]?

I liked that the firm had a non-hierarchical, open-door policy and that partners were approachable. One partner took an hour out of his day to catch me up on a talk I'd missed during the vac scheme due to workload. This kind of generosity towards only a potential trainee made me think the training quality at the firm would be high and I was right. The interview was tough, but I was given great feedback and I learned a lot during that two hours, which to me was another good sign. Lastly the quality of the work was very high across many areas. At that stage in my career I wanted breadth of quality over depth as, even though I thought I wanted to be a competition lawyer, everyone told me to keep my options open.

2. Why didn't you stay with them on qualification?

The competition team didn't have a job opening for an NQ. The team was going through a challenging time with a new head of department and a lot of transitions. Just starting out, I want to be somewhere vibrant, busy and expanding, rather than try to embed in a team that isn't growing.

3. Why competition/antitrust law?

My degree, as you can see, was in international politics. I've always been interested in the EU as a political construct and in international law; it's such an area of complexity and layers. Competition law seems to me to be an area where the political is very present and that shapes the focus of the Commission and the CMA, etc. It's an area where social sciences, politics, economics and commercial practicalities meet, which means there is constant change and growth. To me this is technically interesting and challenging - it's never static.

I enjoyed my seat in tax for some of the same reasons, but as soon as I joined the competition department I felt like someone had switched the light on. I know I have so much to learn, but that's what is exciting. I can't wait to get better and to learn more, build my expertise. It feels really good to have found what I want to do for my career.

4. Why do you want to work for this firm?

I've done my research and see the firm has a stellar award record for being a great place to work, combined with a roster of high-profile clients and cutting-edge work - who wouldn't want that? Based on my reading and discussion with my recruiter it seemed like we could be a good fit. I love my job, I really do. And I want to keep loving it in the long term, which for me means working for a firm where the work is of a high calibre, but where well-rounded associates are valued.

Added to this, joining a small, entrepreneurial-style team where I would have to learn on the go without the benefit of precedents and a huge know-how library, I can see how this will make me a much stronger and more self-sufficient lawyer. It's exciting. Scary, too, of course, but the best opportunities usually are. I know the more responsibility I have, the more invested I am and the harder I work. TeachFirst was like that for me - failure wasn't an option when pupils were relying on me, so I had to get good fast. It's hard to push myself into situations like that sometimes, I know how challenging they are, but I also know the pay off in terms of growth and learning are worth it.

5. Why should you hire me?

For starters, I am passionate and enthusiastic about law and competition law in particular. I have been interested in international law since my A-levels. My father worked for NATO back then and, without fully realising it till recently, I've followed in his footsteps all the way to Brussels. Since I joined the EU & Competition team in my fourth seat I've been so excited to be learning about the EU again and supplementing my existing political knowledge with new legal and economic awareness.

For you this makes me someone who has and will take textbooks home at the weekend to be sure I understand the rationale behind the advice we give and who is genuinely happy to stay late deliver a better service. I still feel very 'new', but I am enjoying growing with each piece of work I complete.

Next, I am determined and hardworking - my partner calls me a 'little bulldog' when I get my teeth into something! I have accepted that my understanding in this job won't immediately fall into place, but from completing my Masters degree and my teaching experience I have learned how to get comfortable with that discomfort, how to step back, read around the area and try a different approach. It's ok to be out of my depth sometimes. I usually find that when it does 'click' I'm more confident in my knowledge than I would have been if it was easy to begin with. I think this is a good skill for a junior lawyer - we can't know everything just yet! In fact someone who thinks they know it all is probably a bit dangerous!

Lastly, and perhaps most importantly, I am a great person to work with and a good team player. I say most importantly, because the other skills - legal knowledge and application - can be taught or systematised, but this one is either natural or not. I'm pleased each of my appraisals at both the firms I have worked at have stated that I'm a generous contributor to my team and a nice person to have around. They've said I excel at the skills that can't be taught so easily - enthusiasm, humour, being willing to pitch in and help out a drowning associate if I can squeeze it in. Clients come back to me in the first instance for smaller matters now, indicating that they trust me to help them, or if I can't, I can find someone who can. I think this generates a network of good feeling.

6. Why law?

I wanted a profession. I've always wanted to be a lawyer and I'm pleased I love it as much as I thought I would. I did detour via TeachFirst[4], but not because I lacked commitment to the law, in fact it was the opposite. I realised I was no different to any of the other straight A, 2:1/first graduates applying for training contracts and that I needed something to set me apart from the crowd. Teaching is still perhaps the hardest thing I've ever done. I learned so much about communicating, handling pressure, not to mention my public speaking skills are great!

TeachFirst also put us through a Masters programme in leadership which hugely enhanced my self-reflective capabilities and made me comfortable handling in-depth research, not to mention a very heavy workload and six-day working weeks. I learned how to be virtually unflappable. I've received much positive feedback on how calm I am under pressure - useful towards filing deadlines - and it comes from teaching. Never let them see you sweat!

Ultimately, I always wanted to be a lawyer, though. Not only do I love the complexity of my chosen specialism, I love that practising law is a mix of intellectually stimulating tasks, commercial practicalities and customer service. I enjoy the rush of a deadline and feeling like our work matters to our clients, that we facilitate what they want to achieve. I find that satisfying. And I'm always

---

[4] https://www.teachfirst.org.uk

learning, never bored. There's so much to get to grips with - it's exciting!

7. Post interview email:

Thank you for an enjoyable and energising meeting. I appreciate the generosity you showed with your time, particularly in light of how busy I know you are.

I'm happy to have had the opportunity to speak with you. I left our discussion feeling challenged, having learned a lot and keen to learn more. I hope I have conveyed that the team you are building is very much something of which I would like to be a part.

I look forward to hearing from you in due course.

HOW TO MAKE A TERRIBLE FIRST IMPRESSION

When I first started as a trainee I believed my supervisor when he said, "If you've got nothing to do, go home at 6". HA. Cut to my first review and, "We feel you're not *aligned* with the department timing." Which is supervisor speak for, "You've been leaving too early".

By coming in at 8 AM and leaving at 6 PM, all anyone saw was me leaving at 6. Because they all started at 9:30. I started coming in at 9, leaving at 7. Cue bonus points for timing in my next review. I was doing the exact same number of hours and just as much work, but no longer had the reputation for being a slacker who wasn't pulling her weight.[5]

This sort of office politics is purely annoying – I mean, surely people should judge you on the quality of your work and whether you meet your deadlines? But sadly, no. They will also judge you on, well, basically everything. And you will soon realise that when you're the one ordering dinner to the office for the third night in a row, your own rational ability to happily wave goodbye to your co-worker at 6 is significantly diminished, too.

These things matter. So, here's how to make a terrible first impression (and what you ought do

---

[5] Well, mostly. First impressions really stick.

instead).

1. Start weak

Don't fall for what I did. Go in hard. Stay later even if you're just reading around the subject area of your new role. I don't mean 10 PM every night, but 7:30/8 PM, depending on the rhythm of your team. As a trainee you shouldn't have to worry about utilisation if your billable/non-billable ratio is low. Make the most of that while you can. Try not to take holiday or get sick (I know, not always in your control, but inasmuch as it is, control it) in your first two or three months.

Let people's first impression be, "Wow, she's really serious about this job."/"He's super hard-working. I better up my game!" Then, when you want to sneak off early in the summer for a pint in the sun, they'll gladly let you go, and the magic of psychology is that they won't allow it to dent their original impression of you much at all.[6]

2. Be nervous as hell

Last week, I was instructing a new intern on a task we'd been set by a partner. Her hands were shaking. She was so worried about saying the 'right' thing that I didn't feel like she could even hear me giving instructions. Similarly, I've lost count of the number of partner doorways I've nervously hovered in, not wanting to interrupt no matter how

[6] Society for Personality and Social Psychology. (2014, February 14). Even fact will not change first impressions. *ScienceDaily*. Retrieved November 22, 2017 from www.sciencedaily.com/releases/2014/02/140214111207.htm

badly I needed something from them.

This is definitely a fake it till you make it scenario. Knock confidently and enter. Ask, "Is now a good time?" If that's too scary, send an email and ask when is best to speak with them, give a specific time window to make it easy.

Take a deep breath and still your hands. Hold something (a notebook and pen should be glued to your hands whenever you leave your desk anyway). Make a note of what you need to say/ask in advance so you don't get flustered and forget. And listen. Take thorough notes, so if your brain is too busy fight-flighting to process what you've been told you can come back to them later.

Remember that we all know the game we're playing. Few people are impressed by the obvious 'keen' response. More will be impressed by active listening and relevant questions.

3. Dress flamboyantly, badly or otherwise deviate from the norm

I'll definitely write more later on this one, but the basic rule is: Don't stand out for your choice of clothing/hairstyle/body art. It's anathema to me but be boring, be ordinary.

Later, once you have a reputation for confidence and solid work, you can add more personality. To the head of my first practice group I will always be 'the trainee who wore that neon dress that one hot day'. He still mentioned it every time he saw me, even two years later. Learn from my mistakes please!

The bottom line is, it makes you look like you

don't understand the culture and you don't **fit in**. Not to sound too Patrick Bateman, but you **do** want to fit in.

4.   Be passive

The biggest gap between school and work is that you now have almost total responsibility for your own progress. You might be passively sitting behind your desk waiting for work, being timid, not wanting to worry anyone, but people will think you don't **care**.

Don't wait for work. Go knock on doors, ask for experience, ask for the context of the work you do get. Ask your supervisor for check-in sessions every couple of months – a sort of status update on your progress – what are you doing well? What do you need to work on? Show that you are actively involved and invested in your career. As in work, so in life, you've got to take care of number 1.

5.   Say no

I once sat with a trainee who turned down an urgent request from a partner to complete a chargeable piece of work, because she was too busy working on a non-chargeable presentation due to be delivered in three weeks. I ended up doing the urgent task despite having two other urgent tasks due and a flight to catch that evening. I mean… **Just say yes**. When you are asked if you have time to take on a task, just say yes. If the deadline between this new item and what you're already working on conflict, say, "I'm working on X for [so and so] right now, let me check if I can move that deadline back at all." Deadlines aren't always as 'dead' as they seem. Good managers will be flexible when they can be.

Of course, if you really, really can't fit both tasks in better to piss off one person by saying no than two by missing both deadlines, but this should really be the exception not the rule. Almost always prioritise the chargeable work. It's how law firms make their money after all.[7]

So if it means skipping lunch, cancelling drinks or working till midnight, when you're just starting out, **say yes**. Be keen. Be helpful. Do it with a smile. Be a team player and when you do want to take an hour lunch or leave early for a party, people will assume you've perfectly managed your time and not that you've selfishly stuffed over the other junior to escape.

Read the other way, here's how to make a great first impression at work:

- Come in a little early; leave a little late;
- Be confident – no you won't know what you're doing, but smile, speak up, make eye contact;
- Dress in line with everybody else;
- Take control of your own progress and learning. Seek out work and experiences;
- Just say yes. And say it with a smile.

---

[7] Exceptions to this might be pitches for new work or slides for a presentation being given the next morning, but they are the exception.

DON'T BE AFRAID TO ASK THE STUPID QUESTION

"*You haven't asked me anywhere near enough stupid questions!*" barked the partner I was working for on the third day of my new job as a qualified lawyer. And he was right. I was paralysed in the middle of information overwhelm. I didn't even know how to figure out **what** I should ask about.

I'm pretty sure I'm not the only person who's ever struggled with this and terrible anecdotal pseudo social science suggests it's likely more common among young women than young men.[8] You don't speak up because you aren't sure whether you should already know the answer. Keeping quiet means not revealing your ignorance a little while longer. Do you look more stupid for asking or not asking?

More on this later, but for now I'm telling you to ask the stupid question. Not appearing engaged or interested, or worse still making a poor guess as to the answer and wasting everyone's time messing up your piece of work is a thousand times more annoying to your co-workers than having to answer a potentially idiotic question. More likely than not,

[8] Speaking While Female: Sheryl Sandberg and Adam Grant on Why Women Stay Quiet at Work, January 12, 2015. Available at https://www.nytimes.com/2015/01/11/opinion/sunday/speaking-while-female.html

it's a perfectly reasonable one and everyone else will be relieved you had the guts to ask, so they can hear the answer, too.

That partner's repeated badgering forced me to get over my anxiety about speaking up and, in his absence, here are some tips to help you do the same.

1. Admit you don't know

When someone directly asks, "Do you understand?" and you don't, SAY SO! If you say, "Yeah, yeah, absolutely," it's thoroughly unconvincing. They know you don't get it, you know you don't and it makes you seem untrustworthy. Your superiors want to know that their work is in safe hands. Just admit you don't know and ask them to explain again. If it's a thoroughly scary and uber-busy partner, try to lie better (they probably aren't paying that much attention anyway) and go find a friendly senior associate to ask.

2. Consider the context

A frequent complaint of more senior lawyers to junior ones is that they don't seem to appreciate the context of the matters they work on. Now, I would argue it's a two-way street and that senior lawyers are quite rubbish at remembering you haven't done this type of deal a hundred times or worked for this client for a decade. **However**, this means that if you start asking questions about where your task fits in the wider matter, what happens next, and so on, you'll be extra impressive and probably feel less lost and more motivated to do your part well now you know people are counting on you.

3. Write them down

When you're reading into a matter or beginning a task on a new topic, write down the things you don't understand as you go along. That way you can look back later and see whether you think you can, or already have, answer[ed] them for yourself. If not, you can take this list in one go and ask your supervisor/the instructing lawyer for input. I used to get flustered, especially when I knew I was out of my depth, and not be able to articulate my query clearly at all. Very irritating for everyone, including me. By writing it down, thinking it through and then clearly asking a thoughtful question, you show yourself to be interested rather than confused. You do need to demonstrate you have applied your own brain to find an answer before you ask to use theirs.

It also means you can cluster your questions and take them all in at once. Interrupting your instructing team member every five seconds will undo all the goodwill your excellent questioning generates. Consider their work as well as your own. Walk the line between keen and nuisance carefully.

The bottom line is: it is okay that you don't know everything, or, as it sometimes feels, very much of anything. You're new. This is hard. There is a lot to learn. And a big part of learning is asking the right questions. Be bold. Curiosity is always better than complacence, especially in a newbie. Ask away!

THE BIGGEST BEAR TRAPS AND HOW TO AVOID THEM

There are some silly, obvious negative behaviours that affect your credibility, particularly when you're just starting out. I canvassed my lawyer friends for the top seven things that drive them crazy when working with new recruits.

1. Typos

This was number 1 of stupid mistakes cited when I took a poll (very scientifically) of all my lawyer friends asking what most annoyed them about instructing junior lawyers. The general gist of the complaint was, why put in all the effort to do the work well and then mess it up by not taking five minutes to proofread it?

Thing is, I get it. You're on a deadline and you've read it through what feels like a **thousand** times and you just want to send the damn thing and go home. But don't. Print it out. Go to the toilet or make yourself a tea and then take it somewhere other than your desk (the library, the secretaries bar, wherever) and go through it with a red pen. You will be surprised how many glaring spelling errors you'll spot or phrases that sound unclear now you're reading them from the page and not the screen. Try reading the document aloud, or in a funny accent. Again, it's simply a silly way to trick

29

your brain into seeing it fresh again. It might take another ten minutes, but better ten minutes late and correct than on time and full of careless errors.

2. Unclear emails

When communicating with clients or asking a fellow lawyer for help or your secretary to assist you, clear email construction is so important. Avoid big blocks of text. Instead, break things down into topics. Use clear subheadings in bold to signal to the reader the focus of each part of your email. Use bullet points or numbers to break up lists or tasks. Used sparingly, bold or underline can be great to ensure the recipient's attention is drawn to the most important information, like a deadline date. I think using it too much is rude, however, so tread lightly.

Read it through at least once before you hit send. It's embarrassing to have to follow up five seconds later because you forgot to mention something crucial or made a mistake. Check you've actually attached the attachment(s) you refer to.

3. Writing memos like essays

A memo of advice for a client is not a law school essay. The same principles apply as mentioned for emails, above. Keep it clear. Keep it as simple as possible. Complex language is tempting when you feel unsure of yourself. The best advice I received about this is to think about it like you're trying to explain the problem and the solution to your Nan (Unless your Nan is a Supreme Court judge.) Basically, someone with no legal knowledge or background.

Always include a summary of your findings and conclusions at the top that the in-house counsel or business manager can easily cut and paste to forward on to their colleagues. Often no one will really care about the complex analysis, they'll just want to know the 'answer'. One partner I worked for used questions as subheadings. Not everyone will like this style, but it did help to keep the client's needs at the forefront of my mind while drafting our response.

If you're drafting a research memo for a senior associate/partner, then you can of course be more technical. But you should still be clear and concise. Keep a record of what sources you consulted and how you arrived at your conclusions. You need to be able to tell them where you looked and what you found in each place so that they can make themselves comfortable you haven't missed anything vital.

4. Taking on too much

This is a tricky one. Really you should aim to say yes to everything. (See above.) But at the same time, you do not want to end up in the situation where you have too much to do and are either late with everything or do everything badly because you don't have time to do it well. Better to have the one person you had to turn away annoyed with you than multiple people whose work is late or rubbish. It is ok to say to someone who asks you to take on a task when you're already stretched, "What takes priority here?" Explain that you have x, y, z for so and so and you're happy to help them, but only if it is ok with that other partner. Often the instructing lawyer will realise you really are busy and find someone else, or they'll support you when you ask for leeway from the other people for whom you're working. It's their call what you should prioritise.

5. Taking on too little

With that said, don't be the idiot who turns down work but skips out the door at 7:30 PM. It doesn't make the best impression, especially if your colleagues are drowning.

6. Working in a vacuum

I confess, I still struggle with this one when it's not my matter, particularly if it's a matter you did not have the good fortune to join from the start. You're given a task, seemingly discrete - a piece of research or a quick piece of drafting - that you complete to the best of your abilities, but somehow, it's just not what the instructing lawyer wanted. You know what you're missing? **Context.** How can you answer the question when you don't know where your work fits in the grand scheme of the deal?

It seems like this should be very obvious to the person instructing you, but as soon as you're the one giving instructions you will realise that it's much harder than you thought to explain the necessary background. So go after it yourself. Help your seniors out by asking questions: Who is the client? What are they trying to achieve here? How do they usually work? What style do they like their advice in? If it's research, what specific facts do you need to know to be able to distinguish useful precedent from irrelevant?

I promise you are not being annoying by asking for extra details. I can't tell you how many times I've heard more senior lawyers complain that trainees just don't seem to appreciate the context of their work (honestly think this is a little unfair - I mean how do you know the context till you've done it a few times? But anyway…). They'll be grateful because your questions will help them shape their instructions. And your work product will be greatly improved to boot! Win.

7. Hovering

I covered this a little already in chapter 2, but don't hover in doorways like a nervous deer. In or out. I absolutely did this as a trainee and it's only when you're on the receiving end you realise quite how annoying it is. It's like you're apologising for your existence. It makes the senior person behind the desk want to say, "WHAT?" in a less than friendly way. They gave you a job; you're allowed to take up space. Just knock on the door, walk in and say, "Is this a good time to discuss [whatever you came in to discuss]?" If it's a terrible time they'll tell you and you can arrange a better one. No drama.

Bonus: Being an entitled asshole

When this came up in our 'Welcome to the Firm' presentation back when I was a trainee, I was surprised. Surely no one genuinely thought they were too good to photocopy things and be polite to the secretaries? How naive I was! A friend of mine told me about asking a trainee to help her with drafting a short letter only for him to pipe back, "Yes but it'd be much faster if you just did it." **Because he didn't want to miss his dinner plans**. She had to explain to him that the client wouldn't pay her rates to do something so simple, and would he mind just getting the hell on with it. Or the intern who refused to prepare drinks for some visiting clients, because that was "the secretaries' job", so the senior associate ended up having to make them. Outrageous behaviour. You're never too good to pitch in. Remember that.

Regarding your secretary if you have one - they've been here a lot longer than you most likely and know a lot more. Having them on your team is such a plus. Be polite and gracious and you have a worthy ally. I promise you don't want them as your office enemy. Word gets around.

EASY WINS: BASIC TASKS

BEFORE YOU SEND A DOCUMENT ANYWHERE:

- Spell check and proofread it.
- Do you need a header? Privilege header? 'Confidential' header? Draft header?
- Does the file name need to be changed to include 'privileged' or 'draft'? Include the date so it's easy to find and you avoid versioning errors.[9]
- Check citation style and footnotes for consistency.
- Check your argument/agreement for internal consistency.
- Check formatting for consistency.
- How do you know what you say you know? Did you just guess? Make sure you have evidence for your assertions.
- Should it be on headed paper to send out?
- Have you actually attached the attachment?
- **Don't send drafts, send your absolute**

---

[9] i.e. When people end up working on old or different versions of a document leading to a nightmare situation of running document compares and trying to make sure the final document contains all the correct information. As the junior, this will fall to you and it's stressful as hell, so we should do our best to avoid it.

best work.

NOW YOU'VE SENT IT:

- What's the next thing that needs to be done? Can you do it?
- If you don't know, who can you ask?

WHEN PLANNING MEETINGS/CALLS:

- Draft the agenda. If it's more informal, send a brief email to all parties letting them know the reason for the meeting/call.
- Have you printed what you and the team need?
- Book the cab (or ask your secretary to do it).
- Share the dial in details with the rest of the team/outsiders.
- Take the meeting note, type it up and circulate it afterwards. Internally first of course. It may not need to go externally. And remember headers (see above)!
- Is there any follow up you can offer to take care of? Did any action points come out of the meeting/call? If so, collect the action points and email them to the team.

SECTION 2: LEVELLING UP

Once you've settled into your new role and mastered the basics, it's time to think about rounding yourself out for the long haul. This section deals with changing the way you think about your role as you progress, taking 'ownership' of your matters and career so you stop thinking of yourself as a trainee and start acting like a lawyer. Your focus will naturally shift as you get away from the 'six-month long job interview' vibe and into the 'rest of my career' vibe. We look at productivity strategies for long-term success, speaking up in meetings, and how to reframe your thoughts when the grind really kicks in.

WHAT GOT YOU TO LEVEL 1 WON'T GET YOU TO LEVEL 2

"The job is what you do when you are told what to do. The job is showing up at the factory, following instructions, meeting spec, and being managed.

Someone can always do your job a little better or faster or cheaper than you can.

The job might be difficult, it might require skill, but it's a job.

Your art is what you do when no one can tell you exactly how to do it. Your art is the act of taking personal responsibility, challenging the status quo, and changing people.

I call the process of doing your art 'the work.' It's possible to have a job and do the work, too. In fact, that's how you become a linchpin.

The job is not the work."
Seth Godin, Linchpin: Are You Indispensable?

When I read the above quote for the first time, I paused for a long second and went back and read it again, and again, till it really sunk in. **The job is not the work.** In that marvellous style that has made Seth Godin, well, **Seth Godin**, he'd just perfectly and simply summed up something I'd been mulling over for years. It's something my first mentor at my first firm touched on in our last meeting and something the partner mentioned at my last appraisal. Like most big points of learning, I had thought I understood it and I suppose I had, on a surface level, but in that one short line - **the job is not the work** - I **got it** like I never had before. Let's break it down a bit shall we?

1. Zero to One

Level 1 is about doing your job. Learning your basics. This level encompasses all the things that no one will thank a law firm for, but everyone will complain about if they aren't in order. No one is really paying you for a perfectly formatted note, they're paying for the advice it contains. But if that formatting is off, if it looks sloppy, then the client won't feel as secure about the advice it contains. They're paying for a professional service and that includes the little things, like perfect spelling and a quick response to their emails. Some trainee basics will include making binders for court or managing the document system in a transaction. They might feel menial and small, but they're the foundation on which everything else is built. You might not feel it at the time, as you're trying to fix a jammed photocopier at midnight, or proofreading a memo for the billionth time, but everyone higher up the chain is counting on you to be their foundation. I had no idea how important this was until I had to trust that the intern on my matter had done her job, so that I could do mine. Saving a document to the system feels like nothing, but everyone working on the wrong version because the last copy wasn't saved correctly could be catastrophic and at the very least an avoidable mega-nuisance. Costing the client an extra £750 because a partner was correcting your formatting errors for an hour is not okay. That's no longer their job; it's yours.

Level 1 is getting these basics down. It takes time. Maybe longer than you'd like it to. It took me longer than I liked it to, but it's got to be done.

2. Level 1 to Level 2

Now it's time to do the work. The real work. Now you know how to format a memo and save a document, prepare an index and take a note of a call, you can start being truly indispensable. As I said above, my first mentor said to me in our final meeting, "Don't lose your personality. That's what will make clients hire you. Everyone expects that a firm of this calibre will get the law right. Client's will stay with you because they like you." I would go one step further and say that this is why a firm will hire you, keep you and promote you.

Level 2 is getting the law right, but more than that, it's getting it right and giving it to the client in the most helpful way you can. When you're just starting out you get props for essentially not screwing up. Now not screwing up does not earn a gold star. It's simply expected. Instead gold stars are earned for doing the little things no one will remember to tell you to do. For me this often takes the form of digging a little deeper than I would have thought to before. Reading a new client's annual reports, finding some academic papers or reports on their industry, building up my background knowledge. It's time spent at the front end that will pay dividends down the road when you can really understand what's motivating their actions or concerns.

Level 2 is asking why you're doing what you're doing, and what the end goal will be. For instance, why are you preparing this note of advice? Practically, to whom will it be sent, or where will the information be used? If it's the general counsel in the first instance, but she is then expected to disseminate the information to her commercial colleagues, then, as mentioned above, make the body of the note technical, but give her a business-friendly top end she can copy paste into her email to them. Remember, the business doesn't love the law like we do. Mostly it's an annoying obstruction. The **work** is thinking, what can I do to make their life easier?

This goes for junior associates with senior associates/partners, too. Anything you can take off their plate, do. Send the note alongside a draft cover email that they can use to send it to the client. When you're managing a long project or research task, send updates regularly so they don't have to worry you've forgotten about it. Set reminders of deadlines whether internal or client ones, and don't be afraid to nudge the instructing partner as they approach. Things do fall through the cracks sometimes. They'll feel better knowing you have their back.

3. Level 3 and beyond

I hesitate to sound like too much of an expert at this point, because I am only wobbling along this boundary myself. But it's here I'm learning to lead as well as be led. And boy, does that ever make it clear where my knowledge gaps lie! Being on the receiving end of all those great questions I told you to ask? Well… it's pretty humbling. But, you know what? It's also been the most rapid period of growth I've experienced as a lawyer. At this point it's about finding your weaknesses and conquering them one by one. It's about becoming self-reliant. I get asked a question and don't know the answer - well let's go away and find out. One more gap filled.

This is also a time for finding the people you admire and learning about them. How did they get where they are? What makes them so great? What can you apply to your work? Level 3 to me will be this cycle over and over - spot a gap, learn how to fill it, embed this skill, find another gap, learn to fill it, embed the skill. And repeat. And repeat.[10] Keep **doing your art**.

---

[10] For more on this principle see -
https://hbr.org/2011/10/making-yourself-indispensable

TAKING OWNERSHIP: YOU ARE THE LAWYER NOW

You are the lawyer now. Not the supporting act. Not the warmup. The actual, real-life lawyer. Remember this. This has been the single biggest mind shift I struggled with – **ownership**. Nobody expects you to single-handedly advise as a trainee. The training wheels are firmly in place – everything goes to your supervisor. Even that three-line email you thought couldn't possibly be marked up.

But now clients will call you directly, you don't have a supervisor, and nothing will annoy your instructing partner more than thinking you've been half arsed with the documents safe in the knowledge they'll catch it and fix it.

This is not easy. Often in a big firm, you are still at the end of a chain of cogs in the deal machine. You won't have been at the pitch or in other negotiations, so you won't know the full background of the client or matter automatically. Moreover, you won't know everything, or really much of anything. Depending on how technical and varied your area of law is, you might just be at the stage of realising the vast and endless expanse of 'things I don't know'. (In which case, congratulations! You've just passed from unconscious ignorance to conscious ignorance and that is actually a great step to take!)[11]

So what can you do? How can you 'be the lawyer' when the only thing you're certain of is that you're not certain about much at all?

1. Get the background

It's the rare instructing lawyer who remembers to state up front a full and detailed background to a task. They all know they're supposed to do it, but they're busy and they forget you don't have access to their hive mind. You've got to ask for it. If they're too busy, ask them to point you to someone else who can fill you in. Without the background context you will either make mistakes, fail to spot something significant, or both. The ten minutes of upfront time will save them plenty more in the long run not correcting your work later.

We've all been on the receiving end of a two-line email asking that you, "Please deal with this" (or the master-level brevity, "Pls deal") attaching a long chain of communication for a matter you've not been involved in, for a client you don't know, so you know just how impossible it is to do a really good job in that circumstance. You need to push back. Advocate for yourself - say you don't know the background and ask where your task fits in the grand scheme of the matter. Ask what has come before and what will come next. This will make your task easier to complete.

---

[11] See the Learning Stages Model at
http://www.gordontraining.com/free-workplace-articles/learning-a-new-skill-is-easier-said-than-done/#

2. Know your client

Once you know the client name, Google is your friend. Read their Wikipedia. Read their website. Check out their annual report[12] and look up any products they have that you don't understand or know about. What do they do? What is their brand? Their corporate message? Check the news – have they done anything noteworthy, good or bad, lately? Have they been in trouble with a regulator or been party to any litigation? Has anything important happened in the industry recently? Be sure to check on their wider corporate group, too, if there is one. Build up a picture of where this piece of work fits in the grand scheme. It's the work of an hour or two, but this knowledge is invaluable. It enables you to tailor your work to their corporate messaging. It makes you look incredibly proactive in the eyes of your instructing partner, largely because that's what you are. Lastly if they're an existing client, find out who in your team works for them regularly. They will have the inside scoop on the personalities involved and the ways of working in the organisation. They may also be able to point you to some examples of previous work carried out for that client to give you an idea of the style and content to follow.

3. Take the work as far as you can

As I said above, nothing is more aggravating to your instructing lawyer than getting the sense you haven't really thought about the task in any depth

---

[12] For US clients their SEC filings will also be very useful.

and have half-heartedly returned it for review expecting that they will pick up the slack and get it client ready. One of my favourite partners has the adage, "Don't send me drafts". Instead start with the mindset that this piece of work needs to leave your hands as client ready as you can possibly make it. No, you won't be able to do as good a job as a partner with 20 years' experience, but do **as much as you can.** Really think about everything that you are writing. Where you are unclear, flag it clearly in the document. It's easy to square bracket a question or something that you're unsure about for the lawyer who will be reviewing your work. This shows you have at least thought about it, even if you didn't know the answer. If anything seems unusual or unclear to you flag that too.

Saying, "I've never done this before" is not an excuse for doing a bad job. If you've never done it before, find out how to do it! We're not at the level where you can use that line to excuse being half-assed.

4. Find out what comes next (and offer to do it)

When you send the piece of work to your senior lawyer, think about what might be next in the chain of actions. If something seems obvious, for instance you have just drafted a memorandum that will be sent to the client by email, offer to draft the cover email to which that memorandum will be attached. This shows that you are thinking through the task and trying to proactively assist your instructing lawyer by taking as much off their hands as possible. If you don't know what comes next, ask. If it's something you think you might be able to help with, say so. If you're not sure, again, simply ask what would be most helpful for you to do next. Partners don't like to feel as though you are underinvested in the matter and just happy to get it off your desk. Show that you want to be involved in the next steps.

5. If you can't help, find someone who can

A wise man and successful business owner I met while travelling through Sydney passed on a piece of advice his equally successful father had given him – "If you can't help them, find someone who can". Nobody likes to hear a dead-end no. If you're absolutely swamped and can't take on another thing, ask around and find someone who is able to do so. If your team doesn't handle the kind of query you just received, find the one that does and put them in touch with the client. It's so simple and takes all of five minutes, but when you're on the receiving end you'll realise how valuable it is as a tactic.

Ultimately the more ownership you demonstrate, the more responsibility you will be given. The more you show you can be trusted with the little things, the more you'll be trusted with bigger and bigger things. And in my experience the more responsibility you have, the more interesting and exciting your job will become.

PRODUCTIVITY AND PLANNING

"Great occasions do not make heroes or cowards; they simply unveil them to the eyes of men. Silently and imperceptibly, as we wake or sleep, we grow strong or weak; and at last some crisis shows what we have become."
Brooke Foss Westcott

This has always been a favourite quote of mine. It is both inspiring and scary to realise that it is the tiny choices you make every day which add up to who you are, not the huge cataclysmic moments. You fall to the level of your training; you don't rise to the level of your hopes. As with life, so with your work. The little things add up. Alone they don't seem like too much, but get this system working and you'll feel in control of your matters, thus leaving more time to devote to the substance of your area of law, instead of always running to catch up.

1. Consistency is key

Can you be counted on? Can you be trusted? Unfortunately in this job, you can be on the ball 19 times out of 20, but that one time you miss will be the one that will stick in the partner's mind the next time she chooses someone to work with her on a new matter. So how can you ensure consistency? Plan for it. Your calendar is your best ally in this.

You should diarise **everything**. When you send something out, set a reminder to follow up in the event you've not heard back. Set a recurring reminder for any tasks you have to do repeatedly. For instance, I have one set to remind me of a board report I have to write on behalf of a client every quarter. This is the easiest way to be sure you won't miss something in the inbox deluge. Sending work to partners before they have to ask for it wins major brownie points.

2. Not every day will be your best day

A very wise mentor I once had explained to 'fresh-out-of-university me' that you cannot be 100 percent, 100 percent of the time **and that is okay**. You will have your 100 percent days where you feel great, bash through your work in a perfect flow state, finish up 14 hours later incredibly proud of what you've accomplished and feeling like a productivity machine! And then you will have your 30 percent days where the simplest email takes 30 minutes to write, you read the same sentence of a judgment 15 times thinking "yes those are words", but without comprehending them at all and filling in your timesheets will make you feel like a monstrous slacker because you have nothing appropriate to say.[13]

These days for me usually follow a couple of 100 percent days. You see, you're actually only human

---

[13] There is no timesheet code for 'twiddling around procrastinating', unfortunately. Though 'personal admin' probably gets abused that way...

and even though we lawyers like to think every day should be at maximum intensity, that simply isn't sustainable. Most days will in fact be 60 to 80 percent days, which is just great. And remember, on those 30 percent or below days, to be kind to yourself.

If you have work you **must** finish that day, break it down into small pieces and baby step your way through it. If you have nothing life or death urgent, then accept that today is a slow day and use the time wisely to set yourself up for greater productivity down the road. Tidy your desk, do your filing, empty your inbox, read those journal articles you been saving. None of this is wasted effort. A good night's sleep and you'll be back in the game, but now with a beautifully tidy workspace and inbox zero.

3. The ever-present to-do list

Most lawyers are list people so I'm going to assume that you fall into that category (occasionally I like to mindmap[14] which really freaks my colleagues out. Wiggly lines! Colours! Ahhh!). Unless it is gone 10 PM and you just desperately want to get home, make sure you take five minutes before you leave each day to bullet point your action plan for the next day. At the end of the day, you will have a much clearer idea of what did and did not get done this day and what is most important for you to tackle tomorrow. This will save you losing the most energetic and productive

---

[14] http://www.tonybuzan.com/about/mind-mapping/

time of your day, first thing in the morning, faffing around figuring out where to start. You can hit the ground running, or, as I like to do, take that 10 minutes to sip your coffee read the headlines and ease into your day safe in the knowledge that last-night-you had it covered.

Your to-do list should be an organic undertaking. Remember to update it during the day as new tasks come in. That sounds straightforward, but you'd be surprised how easy it is to take instructions on something, walk back to your desk, get distracted by something else pressing and forget to write that original task down. The best way to avoid that is to make it habitual that every time you are asked to do something it goes on the list as quickly as possible.

4. The other stuff, the you stuff

Make sure you also diarise and set aside time for your personal development. Try if you can to take at least 30 to 60 minutes a fortnight to stay current in your area of law. By this I mean reading the news alerts and journal articles you should be receiving every day from your knowledge department, or Google news alerts set up for your clients' names, even just checking the headlines each morning. Your day-to-day work will become much more engaging when you can situate your matters in the wider legal and social context.

You should also set aside time every four to six weeks to reflect on how you're doing professionally – is there a type of matter that you haven't tackled yet and would like to? Someone in your team you've never worked with and could approach to get on their next project? An area you feel weak in that you think you should address? It's easy to get your head down and look up six months later to realise that you've drifted off course, you never had a chance to prove yourself and your seat is over/you've been pigeonholed into a certain area. Remember that no one is as invested in your career as you should be, so make sure you give yourself time to reflect on where you have been and where you want to go. You are the captain of your ship!

GETTING YOUR HEAD IN THE GAME

There's a line in one of my favourite films, *Practical Magic*, where after years of trying to hide and ignore that she's a witch, Sally Owens finally has to use her magic to save her sister. She's still pretty mad and scathing of this fact and her aunt, frustrated, tells her, "You can't practice magic while looking down your nose at it." This line stuck with me, because it's something I struggle with (not the magical powers. Are you kidding me? I'd be broom-sticking to work every morning and calling woodland creatures to clean my flat). Lawyers and the culture of law firms can be incredibly self-important: *This is the deal to end all deals! This case will change the legal landscape forever! Bringing in this client will make me partner!* And, yes, sometimes these things are true, but a lot of the time it's just a case of a massive ego and thin justification for missing their child's birthday party.

As a trainee and an NQ it can often feel like your every move is scrutinised. That missing full stop is a calamity and a grammatical error in an email to the client is of world ending proportions. I would find myself thinking, "It's not **that** important really though is it? I mean no one is going to die. No one is even going to care in a week, certainly not a year." Which is true. Very few cases are really ground-breaking, very few pitches career making.

And, let's be honest, at two AM, proofreading a document for the dreaded typo, it's pretty hard to buy into all this self-important, end of the world busyness.

But here's the thing - how you do one thing is how you do **everything**. Your goal as a trainee and an NQ is to learn, to get good, to build skills and networks. And you can't do that while looking down your nose at the system you're now a part of. You don't get to do the big things till you show you can handle the small ones. I'm very much not a fan of the cult of busyness, where people pride themselves on being overworked and stressed out, like the more likely you are to have a heart attack the worthier you are as a human being, sorry I mean lawyer. That is categorically a terrible, terrible attitude to have towards life. I believe firmly in setting boundaries and self-care (more on that later).

However, to get good at anything you have to buy in. You have to do a good job for the joy of doing a good job. A typo isn't just a typo – it looks like carelessness. And if you don't care about checking your spelling, what else don't you care about? That's how you'll make your client feel. So much of being a good lawyer is attention to detail. I know for myself that when I'm disengaged, looking down my nose, thinking, "What is this total bullshit?" That's when I'm not open, I'm not learning. It's when I'm bored and unfulfilled. And it's when I make mistakes.

Yes, a lot of what you will be asked to do as a trainee and an NQ is the decidedly unglamorous side of law. Not for you the two-hour boozy lunch pitches. No, why don't you spend your day making giant perfectly indexed folders of documents that no one will ever read? But, bigger picture, people are relying on you to do that and do it well. Do it well and next time you'll get the slightly more interesting task. Don't check out, don't get snotty and entitled or full of disillusionment. Do your work. Do it well. Use how well you did it as leverage to do something more exciting in future. Remember, looking down your nose at something is just as entitled and self-important as a partner who thinks his deal warrants missing your friend's wedding. It's a bad attitude. Don't have it!

FEEL YOUR VOICE HEARD AND YOU'LL NEVER GO BACK[15]

"Feel empowered. And if you start to do it, if you start to feel your voice heard, you will never go back."
Mary Robinson

It can be very easy, particularly as a trainee, to be a silent presence in the back of every meeting your supervisor takes you along to. Shake hands, sit, take notes, smile, leave. As an NQ, too, I had a hard time shaking off the sense that if I opened my mouth, all I would do was confirm my ignorance, so I kept pretty quiet. I was envious of my contemporaries who could sound off quite confidently about, well, it felt like anything at all. It took a while and some good role models for me to realise that no one knows everything, even if they can sound that way, and further, that it is completely ok not to know the answer at all. It is better to seem engaged and open to instruction, than closed off and disinterested.

I remember being in a meeting as a trainee, listening as a female senior partner, upon being asked a question by another partner answered clearly, "I don't know. It's not my area of expertise, but my suspicion is…" and thinking, "Oh wow.

---

[15] An earlier version of this chapter was published by The Law Society for International Women's Day 2018.

She just said, '*I don't know*' and not only doesn't look stupid, she sounds even more assertive for saying it!" Until that point I hadn't realised that could be done.

Likewise, the QC in a meeting I had last month asked the presenting economist to explain and explain again his point to be sure she caught the nuances. She only looked braver and more in control for her deeper questioning. Comfortable enough in her expertise and intelligence to be fine with her ignorance in this other area. I know that now I, too, have been the only one in the room brave enough to ask the question everyone wanted answered.

It's taken me a few years to get to this point, though. So, if you're just starting out, here are some ways to ease into having your voice heard:

1. Set yourself speaking goals

"I will say at least one thing during this meeting." "I will have at least one opinion on this draft." "I will offer to present a case update to the team at least once a month." "I will ask at least one question about the presentation my colleague has just given."

These goals might seem small to the point of insignificance, but baby steps over time is the best way to build confidence. I know the sting of sitting there, willing myself to talk, only to watch the appropriate moment pass by or hear someone else raise my point. But if you say one thing, and it goes ok, you'll feel more able to add to the discussion next time around. Based on anecdotal evidence[16], it seems that men get just as nervous as women about saying the wrong thing, but they do it anyway. Women, on the other hand, are more likely to keep quiet. So I'm throwing down the gauntlet, ladies, if the men can do it, we can too!

It's important as a junior lawyer to demonstrate you are fully involved and invested in your matters. A partner said to me last week that he actively encourages his juniors to speak up during client meetings to show the client that they are a valuable member of the team and not merely a timid note-taker at the far end of the table.

2. Use the time before the meeting and afterwards

If it's a meeting to discuss a certain agreement or specific matter, then it's easy to plan what you want to convey in advance. Even better if you have time to confer with a colleague and check your understanding is correct. Often, we don't speak up when we're unsure of ourselves. This can't always be helped, but where it can be fixed, fix it! Go through your points with someone you trust, so that during the meeting you can feel confident about your ideas.

Equally, you can always go to your instructing partner following the meeting to ask the question or make the point you had in mind, even if you were too nervous to share it in front of everyone else. This will help build your confidence that what you have to say is worthwhile and it shows them

---

[16] My discussions with friends and colleagues…

that you were switched on, despite not yet feeling comfortable contributing to the group.

3. Eliminate the words of weakness

Every time you find yourself writing the word "just", as in "I was just thinking…", "I'm just wondering if…", **delete it**. It's a word that undermines you and makes what you're saying seem less significant. See how your sentences sound without it. I'll bet it's stronger and more assertive.

The same goes for any kind of equivocation before you speak – "I've only just started to think about this, but…", "You probably know much more than I do about this…". It's a protective barrier between what you're saying and any criticism that you might be wrong. I get it and I've certainly done it, but we must stop. If you're wrong, you're still wrong and those few words won't change that, nor anyone's perception of your mistake. But if you're right, you've just totally undermined yourself and your own opinion for no good reason. Even if you aren't sure of yourself, don't let everyone else know!

4. Feminism alert: Women, politely refuse to be interrupted

Most of my advice is gender neutral, but this is the one issue that affects women more than men. There are plenty of studies about how men disproportionately interrupt women while they're speaking. It can be a real problem, especially if you are already feeling unsure of yourself, or if the man in question is in a position of authority. Obviously, don't blithely shout over the managing partner if he interjects during your piece, but for regular interruptions, you can prepare to handle them. It is ok to calmly and in a measured way, say something along the lines of, "Let me finish up my point and then we can get to yours. Thanks." Smile and be gracious about your power play.[17] There's no reason to be rude or make the other person feel bad for interjecting. But equally, it is perfectly acceptable to stand your ground and finish what you were saying.

To the male lawyers reading this, help your legal sisters out! Firstly, don't interrupt your female colleagues when they are speaking. And back up any woman who needs to request she not be interrupted, as per the above. Pay attention to your current trainee/NQ cohort. Are the men generally more vocal than the women? If you do notice your fellow female trainees or NQs aren't as comfortable speaking out as their male counterparts (accounting for personality, of course), ask them why. If you're more senior, talk with them about ways they can be more involved in meetings, or give them this post to read. Make sure they feel supported and above all, heard.

---

[17] I realise there is a whole host of things to be said about women having to be 'nicer' and never show anger or they'll be disliked. But one battle at a time, ok?

EASY WINS: COMMUNICATION

- Be careful when hitting 'reply all' on emails. You only have to get this one wrong once to get **very** careful about checking who's on the list before you hit send. Especially don't passive aggressively 'cc' partners when accusing someone else of not doing their work or other such rubbish. It makes you look like far more of a dick than them. Mostly because it's a dickish thing to do.[18]

- Equally, do keep people cc'ed on matters that they're working on. There's nothing more annoying than being left out of half the email chains and feeling like you're constantly missing something.

- Say good morning/good evening to people you see when you're entering or leaving the office, including the support staff. It's not nice to make people feel invisible.

- Informality is earned. This means the partner can call you 'mate', but you should not reciprocate unless it's very clear that's ok. Respect travels both ways, yes, but it ought to

---

[18] A partner once corrected my grammar on a reply all email to approximately 10 people. Obviously I've never made that mistake again, but it was an unnecessarily humiliating thing to do to a trainee.

flow much more obviously up the chain of command than down it.

- Don't send someone the piece of work they have to review by nine AM the following morning after six PM. At least not without an apology for sending it late and ruining their evening.
- Get people's names right in emails. So basic right? But I've lost count of the number of emails I've signed 'Katy' only to get back one saying, 'Dear Katie/Kathy/Kate'. It's rude to get someone's name wrong full stop.
- Take five minutes to ask how people are (and then actually listen properly to the answer) before you ask for their help with something.
- Ask if they have time to help you before you ask, too.
- If you know you won't have time to deal with an email query in depth that day, send an acknowledgement email within four hours, saying you've received the message and when you expect to get back to them. No one likes feeling like they're throwing words into a black hole.
- If there's a 'quirky' or difficult person in your new team, ask the existing associates and support staff for advice on the best way to handle them.
- Be somewhat professional on social media, especially entirely public ones like Twitter. Make sure your LinkedIn profile picture is professionally styled as well. That is definitely

not the place for a selfie.

- Turn up to your team lunches, dinners and drinks. Some people act like they're too busy with their awesome life outside the office to get involved, but that's a short-sighted way to be. You should get stuck in and be there. And if you hate your colleagues so much an extra hour with them is unbearable, find another job!

SECTION 3: GETTING PHYSICAL AND GETTING OUT THERE

Your body is where your big legal brain lives, so you need to take care of it and present it well, particularly if it is to cope with the stresses of an intense environment like a law firm. In this section we cover what to wear to work and some simple tricks to avoid developing unhealthy routines (and unhealthy pudge). Instead, I suggest a few healthy habits well worth getting into and some life strategies to lean on when you fall into a crazy busy work vortex. We also look at networking for people who kind of hate networking, what 'business development' really means, and how to handle all the boozing you'll be expected to/enjoy partaking in.

WHAT TO WEAR TO WORK

A long time ago, I wrote a blog post on what to wear to work that went a little viral.[19] Despite obviously being mortifying at the time, I stand by what I said all those years ago so what you'll find below is a slightly updated version of that original piece. And yes, it was supposed to be funny!

Now for what is always the most important question: What should you wear?

Like it or not your clothes make an impression and you don't want that impression to be, "Does he understand how to use an iron?" or "Nice to know she likes red bras." You don't have to be completely devoid of personality, but as with all things in life, you have to know the rules before you break them.

So, the basics…

---

[19]

http://www.rollonfriday.com/Default.aspx?TabId=58&Id=2919&fromTab=58&currentIndex=5; In true tabloid style, they really focused on the important bits…

http://www.dailymail.co.uk/news/article-2452552/City-lawyers-fashion-blog-new-female-recruits-removed-bosses-racy.html; http://metro.co.uk/2013/10/10/berwin-leighton-paisner-city-law-firm-pulls-red-bras-blog-4142189/;

http://www.telegraph.co.uk/news/newstopics/howaboutthat/10368852/No-red-bra-lawyer-dress-code-removed.html

1. Men

a. The suit

Dark blue, charcoal or grey (not too light). Black is only for funeral attendees and bouncers. The material can be fine pinstripe, twill or herringbone, but avoid houndstooth, large checks or wide pinstripes; they belong in the advanced class. You will look better in a less expensive suit that has been tailored to fit properly than a very expensive, but ill-fitting one. Marks and Spencer's is widely touted as the best of the budget brands. Soon as you can afford it, get yourself to Charles Tyrwhitt or Hacketts for something of better quality.

b. The shirts

Fitted white, light blue or pink (for Fridays). Twill not poplin. I prefer double cuff, buttons look a bit 'school uniform', but I can appreciate they are less of a faff, so pick whichever works for you. Avoid checks and stripes; too fussy, particularly if there's any hint of texture to your suit material. Whatever you do, do not wear a coloured shirt with a contrasting white collar. You are not an estate agent from Chelmsford.[20]

c. The accoutrements

Tie colour should complement your suit and shirt. Skinny ties are for Hoxton bars, not the office. Cufflinks should either perfectly match your tie or strikingly contrast with it, no middle ground

---

[20] I'm an Essex girl, so I get to make mean comments about Chelmsford!

here.

Pocket squares should match your tie in colour or pattern, but never both, or alternatively, contrast e.g. blue tie with yellow pocket square. Tie bars should be shorter in length than the width of your tie and worn between the third and fourth button from the collar of your shirt. Choose either a tie bar or a pocket square. Both is just too many things on your person. Pocket square is potentially too much for a trainee altogether, so check you can pull it off without seeming affected.

Keep watches discreet, light faced and silver/steel/platinum. Buy the best you can afford, or don't buy one till you can afford a good one. Don't over-accessorise.

d. The shoes

Always black, not brown, even with a navy suit. No patent, not too pointy. For goodness' sake wear socks.

2. Women
a. The suit

Buy black, three-piece (jacket pencil skirt, trousers in a shape that suits you) and go as expensive as you can. Next and Marks and Spencer's can turn up gems if you look hard enough. If you don't, you will look like a sad Halifax desk bunny from the 80's, so be careful. In time you can upgrade to Whistles and Jaegar.

It is better to buy a size bigger and get it taken in than wear it too tight. Watch for 'smile lines' across your hips, if they appear, go up a size. Do not fall for ASOS or Topshop's 'suit' section. Outside a fashion magazine, a jungle print short suit is not office appropriate.

b. <u>The blouses</u>

You should look to acquire several blouses, say two neutral and two bright, that compliment your suit. Here you can have a bit of personality – zips trims, buttons, asymmetry, pussy bows – but I personally avoid patterns as they tend to look cheap unless they are really high-end. For the same reason avoid satin and anything stretchy. Collared, cuffed and buttoned shirts I've always felt are a little too formal for most women in the office and make you look like a proper 'newbie'. That said, some women can really rock this look, so if you're one of them, go for it!

c. <u>The separates</u>

Get yourself a blazer or bouclé jacket in black, navy and another in a pale neutral, like tan or grey. Aim for at least two to three flattering dresses in colours that go with these jackets.

Don't wear your suit jacket as a blazer – it fools no one and looks sloppy. Dresses should be no shorter than one bic biro's length above the knee[21] and should show no more than a half inch of cleavage if you're lucky enough to have it. My work wardrobe consists almost entirely of smart pencil dresses in various colours and cuts. I find them

---

[21] Full credit to my all-girls grammar school headmistress for that test.

simpler to work with than separates. Just pair them with a complimentary blazer and I'm done.

One black and one neutral (cream, pale grey, nude) round neck, button up cardigan will go with everything and be more comfortable than a jacket when it gets chilly at your desk. Once you have the basics, you can branch out into more interesting colours and styles of knit if you wish.

d. The accessories

Jewellery should be classic(ish, see below) and discreet. Gold, diamond/ante, pearl studs or short drop earrings. A classic, fine bracelet or a good watch. Small rings and no more than two at a time. Wearing all of those together can be too much. A statement necklace may be ok if the rest of your outfit is extremely minimalistic.

Buy a black leather tote bag big enough for an A4 folder and add a tan/nude one once budget allows. Invest in neutral t-shirt bras and non-VPL knickers. Nothing ruins an outfit like bumpy lace showing through your top, or bulges on your bottom. Plain hosiery only; on tights, patterns look especially cheap and fussy.

e. The grooming

If you colour your hair, have regular touch ups. Roots look scruffy and unprofessional. Get a simple cut that you can 'do' in ten minutes and learn a couple of up-dos for days when you don't have time to wash and blow dry (a sock-bun is a lifesaver[22]). Keep your nails short, neat and neutrally polished. A sad fact of life is that most women can look un-'done'; without make up, so learn how to do the 'no make-up make-up' look, even if it's just a touch of concealer, mascara and lip gloss. As with all else, keep it neutral and understated. Do not wear false eyelashes to work. You're not a nightclub dancer.

Lastly, both sexes should invest in a good wool winter coat in black, grey or navy and a trench coat or sturdy umbrella to save nice suits from autumn/spring showers.

Look to the rest of your office for clues on how formal or informal your dress ought to be.

Now you're all set to let your awesomeness speak for itself!

---

[22] https://www.birchbox.com/magazine/article/how-to-sock-bun-hair-tutorial-in-5-crazy-easy-steps

BONUS ROUND: THE FINISHING TOUCHES

The finishing touches are what make you feel 'done', finished, if you will. They have the power to make a bland outfit look polished, or a stylish outfit look messy and ill-planned. Accessories are also where you can have a little more fun with your office wear, I believe. Mine are often little nods to the Converse-wearing, gig-going hippy I am off the clock. A ring made of tiny jet skulls, for example, or a leather trim to my blazer.

My design brief is to keep items small and subtle, so that *I* know the ring is made of skulls and that makes me happy, but I'm not wearing my nose stud and you sure as hell can't see my tattoos.[23] When we make partner we can have visible body art, but until then, keep it covered. You're here to learn, not make a statement.

For jewellery (largely applicable to the women only), as I said above, keep it mostly small and classic. I have rough cut black diamonds, as well as white ones, that are more in keeping with my personal style than pearls would be. But if pearls are 'you', do pearls. Avoid anything that jangles when

---

[23] Note, if you are wearing a white shirt, men, or sheer blouse, ladies, you may want to also wear an undershirt to hide any tattoos. I have made this mistake a couple of times. Minus 50 lawyer points.

you move, for your colleagues' sake. If you have multiple piercings in your ears keep the studs small and elegant. I have a BioFlex flesh coloured stud for my nose piercing while I'm in the office, so it's invisible. If you have pierced ears, men, I'd recommend the same.[24]

Avoid novelty anything, from ties to cufflinks, they always look embarrassing. That's not to say you can't have cufflinks with some personality, provided that personality isn't expressed using any kind of coloured plastic or funny slogan. Brightly coloured socks at the bottom of an otherwise perfectly understated suit is a great look and one I'm pleased seems to be on the rise.

Creativity benefits from constraints[25] and I enjoy finding subtle ways to show my individuality. It's easy to fall into a corporate uniform and that's exactly what you need when you start out, but, bigger picture, what you wear is part of your personal brand (how people perceive you). You'll benefit from making sure it's the right kind of memorable, making you the complete package.

---

[24] I understand that I'm essentially saying, play it incredibly safe and don't do anything not in keeping with the very straight, conservative status quo. I also understand that is quite rubbish for a multitude of reasons, however your first couple of years on the job is not, I think, the time to be making statements and pushing boundaries. Times are changing and I look forward to being a part of that, but establish yourself as credible first. You'll wield a lot more power that way.

[25] https://medium.com/stanford-d-school/want-some-creativity-crank-up-the-constraints-5728a988a635

A note on business casual

Think, lunch with the family at a nice restaurant, not hiking in the Pennines or chilling at home on Sunday afternoon. Despite what you may see from some partners, I don't think sports or leisure wear is appropriately smart. Neither are hoodies, open toed shoes, anything midriff bearing, or ripped jeans. For men, jeans or chinos and a less formal shirt or smart jumper is the right kind of vibe. For women, I like smart jeans, a loose blouse and nice knitwear. You are still at work, after all. And we are still lawyers, not Silicon Valley tech entrepreneurs. You want to look professional, relaxed, but professional.[26]

---

[26] On dress down days, make sure you have a smart outfit stored at the office just in case a client meeting crops up that you need to attend. Worst case scenario you can nip out and buy an emergency outfit. I have done this before in a pinch.

HOW TO AVOID 'ASSOCIATE'S BELLY'

As each cohort qualified at my first firm it would slowly become clear who was experiencing the dramatic step up in responsibility and suddenly working all hours of the day and night. Their shirt buttons would gradually begin to gently strain against their growing tummies – the prize for high billables, little sleep and canteen food for every meal.

We christened this condition 'associate's belly'. The jump in work hours and expectations from trainee to NQ can be a big one and a cosmic storm of exhaustion, convenience and just damn wanting to treat yourself erupts to leave some NQs with a bulging waistline to match their bulging inbox.

Most of these colleagues wobbled (figuratively and a little bit literally) and then got themselves back on track once things calmed down. However, given that cure is always more work than prevention, here are some easy ways to avoid developing associate's belly in the first place.

1. Do not make vending machine trips a habit

Just nipping to the vending machine on a bad day is a slippery slope. Once you've broken the seal. It starts as "only on a bad day", but in times when the days are all bad you become someone who eats a Twix a day. And that's really not a great thing to be. You need to pretend the machine simply isn't there. It's just not a part of your world. It does not exist for you.

Bring small, non-sugary snacks to work. These don't have to be complicated – packets of roast chicken or prawns from the supermarket, nuts, jerky, full fat yoghurt et cetera. Avoid raising and crashing your blood sugar levels - not only does this promote belly fat, but it makes it difficult to sustain energy across a long day and just stresses your body out even more.

2. Drink one of your meals

This might sound a little extreme, but it isn't really. It's an easy way to manage your calorie intake and ensure that you aren't visiting the canteen for breakfast lunch and dinner. I have my bullet-proof coffee for breakfast, a big low-carb lunch and when I can't make it home in time for dinner, a protein shake is an easy option. It ensures I don't overeat, I can keep them in my desk and they don't require any special equipment. Lastly, they're easy to digest which means if I have it late I'm not trying to sleep on a full stomach. It doesn't do to compound a late night at work with a bad night of sleep. Obviously not a long term or everyday solution, but good when you're time crunched and need some form of low-effort sustenance.

3. Squeeze in your workouts when you can

In a 90-hour week obviously please go to sleep! But in a regular long, late week you must find time for something physical. If you want to be in this game long-term you have to stay healthy and active. You need stamina to thrive in such an intense environment. Don't make perfect the enemy of the good.[27] Pick whatever physical activity you will enjoy and you will do. You are much better off doing a half hour of yoga consistently a couple of times a week than deciding to go to the gym six days a week and making it only once.

If I'm completely honest, I fit in my workouts wherever I can depending on the week I'm having. First thing in the morning can be the best during busy periods because nothing can get in the way. My favourite time to work out is lunchtime (as long as I'm doing something like weightlifting where I don't get sweaty enough to require the faff of a shower/make up reapplication), because it breaks up the day and gives me a nice burst of energy for the afternoon. That said I sometimes love to run in the evening as a way of clearing my head of the work day before I go to sleep. In this instance, I often put my gym/running kit on before I leave work, so I don't lose my willpower by the time I get home. You feel much more of a flake removing your kit without working out - having to admit you're not going and peeling it off - than you do not putting it on in the first place. You just need to pick the time that works for you, put it in your calendar like any other non-negotiable appointment and go get it done.

---

[27]

https://en.wikipedia.org/wiki/Perfect_is_the_enemy_of_good

4. Stand and move as much as you can

It's starting to dawn on us just how terrible it is to be sitting down all day[28], so do all the little things you can to get up out of your chair – take the stairs, walk or cycle part of your commute, stand during your conference calls, or go big and beg your employer for a standing desk (this is next on my list). Try to make sure you move at least once an hour. I often set a timer for 45-50 minutes to remind myself to get up, get a coffee, move around a little bit. It also has the bonus of ensuring I can keep my concentration for long periods of time, because I'm taking these little stand-up, refresher breaks.

5. Eat healthy foods before hunger makes you weak

It much easier to say no to the cake your colleague just left at the secretary's desk if your stomach is already full of sushi/salad/chicken. Nobody has enough willpower to resist the constant office temptations when they're hungry. If you have to go for a lot of client meals, take the soup to start (it's well known to fill you up so you eat less in the rest of the meal) and choose the best option you can - steak and seasonal veggies over fried chicken and chips, for instance. Try never to let yourself get desperate and starving. Remember

---

[28]

https://fitness.mercola.com/sites/fitness/archive/2015/05/08/sitting-too-long.aspx

those healthy snacks I mentioned above? They're your secret weapon. Eat good, real food and the tempting snacks suddenly seem a lot less tempting.

GIVE YOURSELF AN EDGE

As you may have already realised, almost everyone you work with is a high achiever. You are now a big fish in a big pond full of big fish. We've already covered some practical ways to make yourself stand out from the newbie lawyer crowd, from asking the right questions through to networking like a real human, now we're going to cover some lifestyle additions that will get your brain switched on at maximum capacity and allow you to function at a high level longer and better than the poor people who don't know about these secret weapons.

1. Meditate

Tim Ferriss, who regularly interviews the world's top performers on his podcast, cites meditation as a common practice for around 80 percent of those high achievers.[29]

If you've been anywhere on the internet lately, you're probably starting to realise that meditation might be a good idea. You don't have to don robes and sit in a cave for 20 years to get the benefits of a meditation practice. For instance, I do 10 to 15 minutes every morning[30] with longer sits at the weekend. Five minutes every day is beneficial and

---

[29] https://tim.blog/2016/11/16/the-tim-ferriss-radio-hour-meditation-mindset-and-mastery/

[30] Okay, *most* mornings… Sometimes life gets in the way.

better than half an hour once a week.

There are a thousand ways to meditate, but when you start out just keep it really simple. Set a timer for five minutes and focus on your breath as it comes in and flows out. Focus on relaxing every part of your body in turn. You could also download a free meditation app which talks you through a very simple mindfulness practice and adds an element of gameplay to building meditation as a skill.[31] If you are open to a more traditional Buddhist practice then I can recommend Tara Brach's wonderfully life affirming and wise podcast for meditations from 5 to 45 minutes as well as hour-long dharma talks full of wisdom for your emotional life.[32]

I confess I didn't realise for a very long time that meditation would have the benefits that it does. I secretly thought that my success came from being driven to succeed by my fear of failure. I was scared that if I calmed down and got peaceful that I would lose my superpower. If you've ever had similar fears, I can reassure you that this is not the case and that meditation gives you the space in your brain to be even more effective. It turns out that the anxiety was not a driver at all but more of a handicap. I also didn't know that the skill in meditating is not in thinking of nothing but in recognising when you've drifted off into a daydream, a worry, a plan, a memory… In those moments when you become aware that you are in a little trance of thoughts,

---

[31] www.headspace.com or www.calm.com, for example.

[32] https://www.tarabrach.com/guided-meditations/

that's when you 'wake up' to the present moment. Every time you do that you strengthen your mind's ability to focus on the here and now. This is where more of the practical benefits of meditation lie.

Imagine how much more productive and creative you could be if you weren't distracted by something a friend did that annoyed you or when you're going to fit in buying your mum's birthday present? If you were solely able to focus on the task in front of you? Achieve the famed flow state?[33] Meditation gives you awareness of, and control over, your thoughts and your impulses. This is a gateway to being a better everything, including a better lawyer.

2. Supplements for superhumans (and some gadgets, too)

Now to be clear, I am neither a doctor nor a nutritionist, but I have tried a lot of pills and potions to enable me to work hard, play hard and train hard without having a breakdown. The items below are what **I** take when I feel I need support in each of the areas I list. I've narrowed it down for you and given you some pointers, but you must do further research to see what you think will work for you. I can only share what has worked for me in the past. Ultimately different things affect people differently. But if these supplements do work for you, they have the potential to be quite life changing. I've included my favourite high-quality

---

[33]

https://www.ted.com/talks/mihaly_csikszentmihalyi_on_flow

brands as a starting point. Don't go to the supermarket or major health food retailers; their products are almost certainly not good quality and likely to be mostly filler. In this sphere you really do get what you pay for.

a. For sleep:

i. *Magnesium* - drinking carbonated drinks, eating sugary refined foods, not getting enough leafy greens, all contribute to low magnesium. As does stress and caffeine consumption. Most people are deficient and would benefit from supplementing. Magnesium activates over 300 enzyme reactions in the body, which translates to thousands of biochemical reactions happening on a constant basis in your body. Magnesium is crucial to nerve transmission, muscle contraction, blood coagulation, energy production, nutrient metabolism and bone and cell formation. All good things, right? This spray before bed will give you the best night's sleep you can remember. Yes, it itches like a mother when you apply it, but it's testimony to its effectiveness that I continue to use it anyway - Ancient Minerals Magnesium Oil.

ii. *5-HTP* - is a compound which gets converted into serotonin in the brain. Serotonin is one of the principal neurotransmitters involved in happiness and anti-depression. It also helps reduce high levels of body inflammation. To aid sleep further you can combine it with a valerian tea or cocoa before bed - Jarrow Formulas 5-HTP.

iii. *Reishi mushroom elixir* - is a potent mushroom used frequently in Chinese medicine for everything from improving immune function to fighting tumors, but it also aids relaxation especially if you take it consistently over time - Four Sigmatic Reishi Mushroom Elixir.

iv. *Ice bath or cold shower* - this has a surprisingly soporific effect! 10 minutes if you can handle it and you'll sleep unbelievably deeply.[34] I found it especially effective in the summer when being too hot made it impossible to sleep. A two-minute cold shower at the end of your normal shower in the morning has also been shown to have amazing mood boosting properties. You'd think it would make you grumpy as hell but it's the opposite!

v. *Sleep Master sleep mask* - this soft satin mask wraps fully around your eyes and ears so it doesn't fall off like most masks. The change in sleep quality since I started using it is unbelievable. It may be the best £20 I've ever spent. I take it every time I travel.

b. To manage stress:

[34] https://tim.blog/2008/01/27/relax-like-a-pro-5-steps-to-hacking-your-sleep/

i. *Rhodiola Rosea* - is an adaptogenic herb (a nontoxic medication that normalizes physiological functions disturbed by chronic stress, through correction of imbalances in the neuroendocrine and immune systems) that has been shown in clinical studies to help combat "21st century stress" - tiredness, brain fog, low energy and sadness - Solgar Balance Rhodiola Complex.

ii. *Krill oil* - I started taking this to help combat some mild depression I suffered a few years back. Fish oil reduces inflammation, improves brain function and helps boost your mood. It's extremely important to find a high-quality brand and keep it in the fridge, as oxidised fish oil is worse for you than no fish oil - Jarrow Krill Oil.

iii. *L-theanine* - this is especially useful if you've been leaning too heavily on the espressos to stay alert. It is an amino acid found in tea leaves. It neutralises the anxiety inducing effects of caffeine and promotes relaxation by boosting brain calming chemicals, lowering 'excitatory' brain chemicals and enhancing alpha brain waves. It's relaxing without sedating - NOW Foods L-Theanine. Kimera Koffee also contains L-theanine (among other things) so you can get your caffeine without the jitters.

iv. *Vitamin D alongside vitamin K2* - a must if you've

been inside for all the daylight hours for all of the days. Vitamin D is one of the most important supplements you can take and almost everyone is deficient. It acts on over 1,000 different genes and serves as a substrate for sex hormones like testosterone, human growth hormone, and estrogen. It moderates immune function and inflammation. It assists in calcium metabolism and bone formation. Take it in the morning so it doesn't affect your sleep and take it with Vitamin K2 as there is some evidence supplementing vitamin D without K2 can be pretty bad for you[35] - Betteryou Healthy DLux 3000 Oral Spray and Life Extension Vitamin K2 or Betteryou make a combined spray of D and K2.

v. *Chaga mushroom elixir* - it tastes like dirt, really just awful, but it's the thing to take when you feel like you might be getting sick and you really don't have the time to be under the weather - Four Sigmatic Chaga Elixir.

vi. *Ashwaganda* - another adaptogenic herb, this time one that can cure almost anything if the internet is to be believed! That said it is effective in me at least for relieving stress by lowering cortisol levels - Simply Solgar Ashwagandha Root Extract.

---

[35]

https://articles.mercola.com/sites/articles/archive/2013/10/19/vitamin-d-vitamin-k2.aspx

c. <u>For mental focus</u>:

i. *Choline* - Choline is needed in order to make the neurotransmitter acetylcholine, which is required for cognitive and muscular function and memory. It's one I can really feel if I miss a day, I just feel foggy headed and less able to think clearly - Nature's Way Choline.

ii. *Lion's mane mushroom elixir* - I can't say enough good things about this product. You just have to try it. Its effects are intense and amazing. Lion's mane has been referred to as a "smart mushroom," providing support specifically for cognitive function, including memory, attention and creativity. It stimulates synthesis of Nerve Growth Factor, a protein that plays a major role in the maintenance, survival and regeneration of neurons in both your central and peripheral nervous systems. One cup of the tea and you will feel the difference all day - Four Sigmatic Lion's Mane Elixir.

iii. *ALCAR* - or Acetyl L-Carnitine for long, is used as a brain booster, due to its ability to increase alertness and mitochondrial capacity while providing support for the neurons. ALCAR is an amino acid that is found naturally in the body, but supplementation can help with memory and cognition – Boom Supplements Acetyl L-Carnitine.

iv. *Qualia* - the granddaddy of nootropic blends, this is not cheap nor for the faint of heart. It contains an enormous list of cognitive and mood boosting ingredients so long it has to be split into two doses of nine horse-sized pills to get down. That said, short of Modafinil, it's the strongest stuff around and has a markedly noticeable effect.[36]

I don't take all these every day, just when I intuitively feel I need them. If I've not made it out in the daylight all week, I'll be sure to take vitamin D. If I know I've got to rack through three brain-intensive tasks in one day, I'll have a lion's mane tea. If my sleep's been disrupted, I'll take some magnesium before bed. Learn to recognise what your body needs and treat it kindly. You deserve to be taken care of by yourself.

It's also worth noting that these are the top 20 percent additions to an already healthy regime. Nothing in this list will counteract consistently poor sleep patterns or dietary choices. Before you drop hundreds on the above, tackle the low hanging fruit - get eight hours of sleep a night, eat more vegetables, eat less processed rubbish and go for a walk. Of all these, just getting enough sleep will make a ridiculous amount of difference.[37]

---

[36] http://neurohacker.com/qualia/
[37] https://thoughtcatalog.com/ryan-holiday/2015/07/heres-your-productivity-hack-go-the-fck-to-sleep/

NETWORKING FOR THE SOCIALLY AWKWARD JUNIOR

It's your first business development breakfast meeting. It is far too early to be socialising but somehow you need to make great, engaging small talk with your clients' in-house counsel while trying not to get croissant crumbs down your tie. I bet you're nervous. I know I was. See also: uncomfortable, and terrified of saying the wrong thing. So, I did a little digging into the dreaded 'networking'. There is **a lot** of bland, boring and banal advice out there and I promise not to add to that pile.

I'm going to assume you already know not to have a limp handshake and that you should make an appropriate amount of eye contact when you're speaking with someone. That's the foundation stuff. We're going to look here at the things that take you from "not an horrific embarrassment to the firm" to, "Who was that charming young associate I just met by the coffee?"

Kidding! They'll know exactly who you are, because you'll have given them your card.

1. Be nice and polite to *everyone*

You are an extension of the firm. How you act reflects not only on you but on the firm as a whole. Be as polite to the guy checking your coat and giving you a name badge as you are to the keynote speaker. That means eye contact and a smile for everyone. Don't be dismissive. This isn't the easiest to do when you're in a rush, but it doesn't take long to make someone feel seen. Say thank you. I know I said I wasn't covering the basics, but I've seen too many people (*cough* very senior partners) completely ignore serving staff, or even trainees. Hint: you're not better than everyone because you're in a nice suit or the higher rate tax bracket. Don't be rude. Treat everyone respectfully. If you need more motivation to do that than simply being a good human, remember you never know who someone is or when you might have to interact with them again.[38] So be nice. To everybody.

2. Be honest but not self-deprecating

When you're just starting out it's completely acceptable to admit that. Don't try to hold court on all the fancy deals you've been involved in, when all you've really been doing is making folders of documents and photocopying. It is a much better strategy to dig into someone else's expertise. Say you're a trainee or an NQ and you're interested in <u>their opinion on X, Y, or</u> Z. Good questions

---

[38] This goes too for conversations you have in lifts, or bathrooms, or any shared area in your firm. You never know who those 'strangers' are that are sharing the space with you, so it's pretty sensible not to badmouth anyone or have a whinge session about being made to miss your dinner plans tonight. Said stranger may very well be the head of a department you don't know well or a consultant VIP and you will have just made a terrible first impression on them. Discretion is the better part of valour and all that...

include:

- Why did you come to this event?
- Which speaker are you looking forward to hearing from and why?
- What is the biggest challenge in your role?
- What do you wish you knew when you were at the start of your career?

Think of everyone you meet as a repository of interesting information. Ask the questions and really **listen** fully and presently to the answers. When you network like this it feels real and creates lasting bonds. Honest and genuine interest will really engage people and warm them to you.

There is one caveat. Be honest, but don't be self-deprecating. Don't say, "I'm a trainee what do I know?" Don't make the person that you're speaking with feel like they should be engaging with someone more influential. You are a professional; it is okay to act like it.

3. Know your target demographic

Everyone has a target demographic of people with which they generally do well talking. And also one with whom they struggle. Now obviously I'm making sweeping generalisations here, but sometimes it's got to be done. Most people will be the most comfortable approaching others of the same sex and/or status as they are. It's much easier for me to approach a group of young, female junior associates than older, male partners. In all honesty,

I think this works both ways.

Without wishing to sound like I'm giving pickup artist advice, it's often best to look for someone by themselves, probably equally nervous, and introduce yourself to them, rather than interrupt the flow of a group conversation. And if you're the lucky one ensconced in the group, indicate with your body language or eye contact and a smile, that you're happy for newcomers to join you. Above all, be kind and welcoming whenever that's an option.

4. Prepare, but think on your feet

When attending a talk or networking event you ought to have some inkling of the topic and likely interests of the people in attendance. Attendance lists are usually circulated before the event, so it's a good idea to quickly Google people and their respective companies so you know your audience and can tailor your questions and conversation to their areas of expertise. For instance, it's probably best to avoid launching into a diatribe about how you've just finally seen *The Constant Gardener* and are **outraged**, only to realise you're in a room full of big pharma executives…

When speaking with in-house counsel, having some knowledge of their business and the issues affecting them and some curiosity about what's important to them will go a long way in endearing you to them. Don't however, attempt to tell them what **you** think is important, unless they ask. You're not an expert yet, they are. As Ernest Hemingway said, no one listens anymore. Allow the conversation to flow by really listening to what's being said rather than trying to squeeze in the **really important and clever thing you desperately want to say** so you can sound intelligent. Listen when people are talking. Don't plan your next point. Let it flow. It'll feel better for everyone.

5. Follow-up

Make sure you take a card from the people you meet, or make a note of who they were, and send a short follow up email. Nothing fancy, just, "It was a pleasure meeting you yesterday". Perhaps you can add a link to an article on something you spoke about. Say you look forward to seeing them at similar events in future, or, if you particularly hit it off, to be in touch if they're ever in your city and would like to meet for a coffee. Be the one to go first. People rarely do this and it makes a real impact. Everybody likes to be courted.

REMOVING THE MYSTERY FROM BUSINESS DEVELOPMENT

As a trainee and NQ, you're most likely to log your time as 'BD' when researching news stories on a company for a partner who's about to meet them for lunch, or preparing a pitch presentation, or completing a complex and time sensitive request for tender. It's a bit of a catch-all for any work that isn't chargeable to the client, but that might help win chargeable work in the future. Often, it's treated a bit resentfully as work you have to undertake, but that doesn't count towards your chargeable hours targets.

Business development as the practice of bringing in new clients, new work from existing clients and relationship building with current and potential clients often feels quite mysterious to junior lawyers. I was so concerned with doing my basic tasks to the correct level and simply keeping my head above water that I confess I didn't even think about how to 'do' BD until at least 18 months qualified. And I think that's ok. This is definitely a level 3 skill in the junior associate toolkit. It's where networking meets marketing and it requires that you know enough of both your firm and your practice area to be able to promote either in a meaningful fashion.

This is also an area where it's likely the size of

your firm will play a role in determining how proactive you can be at your level. A smaller firm will mean you'll have more leeway to get involved in BD and probably more encouragement to do so as well, as it's all hands on deck when there are few of you to share the load. A larger firm may well have a full team dedicated to promotion and marketing, be much more tightly controlled about client access and want its juniors billing hours at their desks, not out schmoozing potential patrons. That said, you should think about balancing the wishes of your firm with your long term personal career goals, because having clients loyal to you and the skills to bring in new business is what will give you the most clout down the road to partnership (or wherever else you want to be).

I'm not a sophisticated marketing machine, nor do I think at this level as lawyers, we must be one. What I set out below are a series of pointers to get you thinking about business development at a high level. I can almost guarantee that if you start asking questions about client relationship building and showing an interest in real BD at this point, you'll mark yourself out as 'one to watch' in your trainee/NQ cohort. I don't know about you, but I cannot *wait* to bring in my first paying client!

1. Know your competition

What firms in your location also have teams dedicated to your practice area? This is pretty simple if you're in corporate finance (pretty much all of them), but if you're in a niche area, like Art, the playing field may be quite small. Use Chambers

& Partners and the Legal 500 rankings to get a sense of the top firms and the type of work that they are doing. Who is doing the type of work you (and your team) want to be doing? How are they landing these clients? For this you can look at their websites to determine the language they are using in their promotional material. Read the legal press (The Lawyer, Law360, Legal Cheek etc.) to find out what other firms in your niche are working on.

What distinguishes these firms from yours? What distinguishes your team from the rest of the market? Do you know what your firm sells itself on? If not, ask! I know that my team right now are specialists in a particular type of claimant side litigation, having had huge success in the US with such cases. They leverage this success and experience to obtain more work in this niche area. While they of course take on wider work in the competition field, this is their USP (unique selling proposition).

2. Know your target

I've covered before the sorts of material you can use to learn about client (or potential client) businesses – annual reports, Form 10k's, websites and promotional material. Also look for trade associations of which they are members. Are these associations carrying out any lobbying activities? This could give you an idea of what is important for the industry right now. Searching the press for stories involving their industry and competitors, will also help build a background picture for you.

When looking at material either produced by the

company, an association they are involved in or even quotes from their business people in newspapers, consider the language they use to describe themselves and the problems/challenges they are facing. This attention to detail will enable you to communicate with them on their level. Using the language that they use and demonstrating a real understanding of their business is lightyears more advanced than trying to sell someone on why *you're* great and so is your firm. A commercial person with a problem to solve is only going to care about your firm capabilities in as much as you can show that you are capable of fixing their problems and enabling their business to succeed. You should get very clear on your target and what they want to hear. It should be all about them, not you.[39]

3. Promotion comes in many forms

The ultimate aim with media coverage of any kind is to become a thought leader for your area of expertise or interest. This means you are the person people turn to when they need a quote of an article (or legal advice) on a particular subject. Now, you might not know what that is yet, but it's good to be bearing that in mind as you progress. Be on the lookout for the issue that takes your fancy. In the meantime, you can practise your burgeoning BD skills across these three areas:

---

[39] For more on this principle:
https://www.iwillteachyoutoberich.com/the-briefcase-technique/

a. Reference materials

Bigger firms will, as I said, have departments devoted to producing glossy materials on topics of interest for the firm website and to send to clients. If you're at one of these firms you can offer to get involved by bringing topics to the BD team's interest, writing case reviews for them and so forth. See if there's scope for you to help them out with their next publication. They're often desperate for lawyers who want to be involved in creating content for them, so you'll be very much helping each other out.

If you're at a smaller firm, offer to produce standard pitch documents if they don't have them on file. A capability statement (like a CV for a law firm, usually focused on one commercial area per statement, e.g. telecoms or media) is a great place to start. Firms often have old precedents they've used in the past, that you can offer to update and refresh. It a great way to learn more about your team's past work, too.

b. Expert commentary

One of the first business development practices you can get involved in as a junior is publishing articles in law journals. To start with you may simply do the first draft of whichever article your supervising partner has been asked to produce, but as you get more experience you can push to write on a certain topic or in a niche area and try to establish yourself as an expert in that subject. I've been very clear that I love writing, so when an opportunity to publish comes up my name is top of the list of associates to tackle the piece. This is a very accessible way to get your name out there. Partners need to do this kind of promotion, but it's quite time intensive, so they'll be grateful if you offer to draft them something that they can work with. Ask if you can be listed as co-author. Most partners worth their salt will do this automatically, but if not, it pays to be pushy.

c. Press

Being an expert in the legal journals, to other lawyers, is one thing, but becoming the 'go to' expert for the mainstream press is another entirely! Now this perhaps seems like a more senior associate and partner level skill, but that doesn't mean a) you can't help them make connections and b) you can't start thinking about it now, so you're in pole position when you're comfortable taking the plunge.

The secret is, everyone in the press is desperate for content. They need leads and stories to write about every day, so if you have something interesting to cover, like a change in legislation that will affect certain businesses, find out how to get in touch with journalists that will be interested in writing about it and contact them with your story angle. For press attention the story has to be timely. Certain times of year really lend themselves to obvious angles, too. For instance, suggest things like 'top ten developments' lists at year end.

You can start with small publications, like trade journals, before you go pitching the Financial Times. Twitter is a great place to join the conversation with the media, as is LinkedIn. Most papers have contact details listed prominently on their websites, too. Internet based news outlets, like HuffPost, are always on the hunt for new material. Guest blogging is another brilliant outlet possibility. Don't be shy! And once you get published be savvy about pushing the use of social media to promote yours and the firm's efforts. This is an area where us millennials can definitely help lead the way.[40]

4. Relationship building

Another great place to find potential clients are conferences and trade associations. Lawyers love to conference with other lawyers and that's great, but it's not likely to be where you find clients. Conferences on the business specialisms you're interested in, however, will be full of experts you can learn from and business people who may need your advice. For conferences, study the agenda ahead of time, research the speakers and panellists, so you can be targeted about where you spend your energy. Introduce yourself to the ones who impress you (flattery will get you many places). Follow up with them on LinkedIn.

Associations can also be virtual. In this instance, follow the stories and discussions. Chip in if you have something of value to add, or a good question to ask. Be clear before you start about your message – who are you and what can you offer? It's better to

---

[40] Do make use of your firm's BD and media officers here, though. Don't just go tweeting in the firm name. That's dangerous territory for juniors.

be a specialist than a generalist for business development. For instance, I might say that I'm an antitrust lawyer with a focus on payment systems litigation and fintech advisory work. Not that I'm just a competition lawyer; it's too broad to allow someone to decide if I'm helpful to get to know or not. This is different from general networking. You're positioning yourself as an expert in a niche. The go to person for that area.

With clients and the press, the ultimate goal here is to build relationships that lead to business. As I said above, to do that you should start with the other party, not with yourself. What can you offer to make their life easier? How can you help them achieve their goal or be better at their work? Pitching a journalist a really great story or keeping an in-house lawyer ahead of the curve on changes to the law that will affect their business are great places to start. This gets easier the more you get to know the other person/business, too. You'll start to really understand what they want and how you can best support them. You'll become the trusted advisor they turn to when they need help and, even better, the person they recommend to their friends and business contacts next time they're asked.

Consistency is key, again. We're playing the long game here. Keep being a useful person to know, keep offering valuable assistance, keep building your profile in your specialist area. Don't wait months between efforts. Try to make this a regular part of your practice. I've diarised a 30 minute block every Wednesday to strategise my BD efforts.

This week I'm off the hook, because I have an article to draft for a high-profile journal, but when that's over, I'll be back to LinkedIn discussions, searching for useful conferences to attend and news about my best clients' industries. Baby steps. This is a skill like any other. Awkward as it feels now, we'll get it soon. And far sooner than those who don't even think about it till senior associate. Onwards!

HOW TO DRINK WITHOUT EMBARRASSING YOURSELF

Being a trainee can sometimes feel like being on a two-year freshers week. You are expected to participate in graduate recruitment events and these will almost certainly involve drinking large quantities of dreadful, cheap wine without any dinner to soak it up. Then at interview and onwards you will attend networking lunches, dinners with colleagues, leaving dos and a myriad of other social events that will require you to either hold your alcohol well or stealthily abstain.

Now some of how you handle this will depend on the firm and the team you're working in. In some types of teams (naming no names... corporate finance... banking... ahem...) borderline alcoholism appears to be positively encouraged. In other less flashy areas such as my own, EU and competition, that kind of behaviour will likely be very out of step with the rest of the team's attitude. Whatever situation you're in, there will be times you will need to find a balance between being outgoing and sociable and being an embarrassing liability. These are just a few tips and tricks to keep you on the right side of the dividing line.

1. Eat something!
I know, I know! You already know this one. But

how often you'll actually remember to do it is a totally different matter. Graduate recruitment events in particular always seem to start at five or six PM leaving you trying to politely cram as many crisps for dinner into your mouth as you can possibly get away with amidst conversation. An empty stomach plus three glasses of budget wine is a recipe for regret!

The best thing to do is to eat something filling and fatty before you go to the event in question. Avocado on toast, covered in olive oil and a bit of salt and pepper is a perfect pre-gaming snack. A couple of hard-boiled eggs, a packet of salmon and mayonnaise, that sort of thing.[41] Obviously in a pinch, a sandwich from Boots will suffice, but there are a lot of better offerings around these days, especially in London. You just need to get something fatty into your stomach before you fill it with alcohol.

2. Drink clean

At certain events, you won't have much choice about what you can drink. It will be red, white or beer. In this instance pick whichever one you know you can drink the most of comfortably without it showing. I found white wine topped up with a little sparkling water by the barman was the best option for me. I know many people choose the beer in this example. If you go for the red wine remember to

[41] https://tim.blog/2015/08/26/how-to-build-a-world-class-network-in-record-time/ - Tim Ferriss (yes, I do really love him) gives a lot of tips on surviving boozing and networking events in this talk.

check your teeth from time to time in the mirror. Red wine mouth is not a great look when you're meeting people for the first time.

Where you have a choice, go for clean alcohols. By this I mean clear spirits like vodka, gin, tequila (not the cheap stuff). These spirits mixed with soda, tonic or nothing respectively will give you the nicest booze to hangover ratio. Avoid anything full of sugar like Sambuca (I mean to be honest avoid that anyway, just on principle) and any mixers full of caffeine that will keep you tossing and turning when you eventually do try to go to sleep. Do remember to drink some water between rounds. Again, I know you know this, but I also know that almost nobody does it.

Lastly, do know when you have had enough and should call it a night. Everyone has their own tells. Weirdly my face goes slightly numb when I've had too much to drink and that is a warning sign that I need to leave immediately. Don't be the person who has lost the power of speech and definitely don't be the person pulling a vac schemer or throwing up on the dancefloor.

3. What to do if you can't, or don't want to drink

Most importantly, don't make a fuss about it! Rightly or wrongly people will assume a) you're boring and b) you're judging them. A good trick is to simply take the drink and then not drink it. Tip a bit away when you go to the toilet, or just put the glass down somewhere when no one else is looking and get yourself a soft drink. You can also offer to be the one to get the next round and order yourself a soda water. Ask the bartender to add a lime and pretend there's vodka in it if anyone asks. Obviously, these options work best for when you're with people you don't see often, or for the occasional times you aren't drinking for whatever reason (an early workout the next day/you're taking antibiotics etc, etc.).

If you don't drink ever and you're with people you will see frequently, again don't make a big deal out of it. Turn down the offered alcohol, get yourself a soft drink and change the subject. You don't owe anyone an explanation and the more you do explain the more awkward it will be. Do remember however to still get involved in the fun. A lot of this job is about being liked and being sociable. In our society, rightly or wrongly, a lot of this revolves around having a drink at the end of a long week or long deal. You definitely don't have to drink, but it will pay to get involved in the social side of things. And I don't just mean career wise - some of my best friendships were forged on drunken trainee nights out to terrible City bars.

4. The next day

Show up. And look presentable. Calling in sick with a hangover is absolutely and completely unacceptable. You are a professional adult with responsibilities. Being too hungover to come into work the next day is just flat out not okay. It may even be a disciplinary matter at some firms if you're found out (and the rumour mill will almost always out you). Of course, you won't be at your best, but you must be there. Plus, it's a great chance to bond with your partners in crime as you struggle through the day together. Be the hero that suggests a full English in the canteen or brings in a dozen Krispy Kreme for morale. But above all be there.

KEEPING YOUR SH*T TOGETHER WHEN YOU WORK THE CRAZY HOURS

Eighty-hour work weeks are only glam and exciting in the confines of a John Grisham novel. In the real world, when you're not saving an innocent man from death row, they just feel like a never-ending march towards braindead zombie-dom. And it doesn't always have to be 18-hour days to make you feel like you're losing grip on life, a solid fortnight of post 10 PM finishes is enough to tip the balance from manageably busy, to miserable grind. The washing piles up, you can't find a clean spoon for your breakfast, your friends are mad you've missed every get together for ages. It's going to happen. We get the money, the nice offices, the excellent career progression all for the price of some late nights and missed parties. Fair game. But I am more resentful of this fact when it feels like the rest of my life is being sacrificed to the gods of the office. If I can keep my personal admin under control I feel like a plucky young associate making her mark in the big City rather than a panicked, frazzled mess with too much dry shampoo in her hair.

A quick point before we get to the listicle – insane hours are not a given, even in the City. Hours expectations vary both between firms and in different teams within firms. It's up to you to choose what works for you. Some people absolutely thrive on being mad busy all the time, others like quietly contemplative, solid work. I'm somewhere in the middle – I love intense patches as long as I know there will be some down times. Find a pattern you can deal with. Yes, your twenties and thirties are the time to pay your dues and work your ass off, but life's too short to be desperately unhappy for too long. You don't have to love, love, LOVE your job, but you should really like it and you definitely shouldn't hate it.

1. Outsource everything possible

Get your shirts ironed by the dry cleaner, order your shopping online, hire a cleaner, and so on. Now is the time to throw money at any problem you can to take some of the pressure off yourself.

2. Quick healthy meals

Avoiding eating your three square meals in the canteen or nearest coffeeshop. It'll only make you gain weight and get tired. Toast and peanut butter, scrambled eggs with spinach and a bit of garlic, or rice noodles and some packaged stir fry veg all take two minutes to prepare, but will make you feel much nicer than eating cereal or the reheated greasy offerings in the canteen at 10 PM for dinner each night. Think of yourself as an endurance athlete - you've got to go the distance and that means fuelling yourself correctly. Red Bull and chocolate will have you burning out and crashing way before the finish line and we don't want that.

3. Take 10 when you can

If you've just sent the documents to the other side and you now have a few hours while they review them, then take that time while you can and step outside for some air. A walk round the block really can help clear your head. I used to get really nervous about leaving the office outside of lunchtime, but no one is hawk-like watching your whereabouts anymore. If you can take a short break, do it!

4. Treat yourself

One of the best things I ever did during a particularly insane patch was to take my allotted four hours off on Sunday afternoon and get a massage. It would have been much easier just to flop on the sofa at home, but walking the short distance into town and having someone soothe my aching back for an hour was priceless. Even more so than having all the kinks worked out was the feeling of looking after myself. Being stroked is not just for cats. A manicure, a facial, a swim in the local pool, even a trip to your favourite ice-cream parlour, all will remind you what it's like to feel human.

5. Get clarity on what's expected

When juggling deadlines and overwhelm, it's good to get really clear about what needs to be completed and by when. It may save you unnecessarily staying up all night on something where the deadline has been moved or the task is no longer relevant. Sometimes deals move fast and people might not always remember to let you know. Just make sure when you ask it's in the context of wanting to meet the deadlines and doesn't sound like you're whining about staying in the office late. It's a tricky line to walk, I appreciate.

Overall recognise that you want to be in this for the long haul and try to manage yourself accordingly. I've heard too many stories of people who loved law but left after their training contract because they worked somewhere that took a "burn 'em and churn 'em" attitude to trainees and NQ's. Your career has to be, to coin an overused phrase, a marathon not a sprint. During your training contract you do, to an extent, have to go all out each seat, because it is basically a six-month job interview. But once you qualify it's more up to you how you manage yourself and the firm's expectations. There will always be times when things get astonishingly busy, but at most firms worth working for, if you're in the office till eleven every night (especially if you're the only one), something has gone wrong and you should speak to your supervisor or a trusted partner. I'm serious about doing this job long term. I don't want to burn out. Anyone worth having as a boss will see it that way. And if they don't? Well there's no shortage of law firms in the UK. Go find one that does.

WHAT I WOULD TELL MY NEWBIE SELF: SUGGESTIONS FROM MY PALS

I canvassed my favourite lawyer friends and colleagues for their best responses to the question, 'What's the one piece of advice you would give to yourself, if you could go back in time to when you'd just started out?' Here is what they shared:

- <u>If you think of yourself as 'just a trainee' then that is all you will be. You can be as much as you want to be and should approach work in the same way – imagine yourself as an associate in each department and be one (without being too arrogant!)</u>

- The little things matter. Don't rush. Double check everything, especially at the beginning.

- Ask all the questions you need to and then make sure you listen to the answer. Any (good) supervisor should have time for all of your questions the first time round.

- Treat all the research notes that you do for other members of your team with the same amount of care as if you knew they were going to a client.

- Put every important deadline in your calendar and set appropriate reminders. Do the same for when you should you follow up with e.g. a client who promised to send you something. This way nothing slips through the cracks and you're in control of your matters.

- <u>Never send an email when you're angry. To paraphrase Warren Buffet, you can always tell them to go to hell tomorrow.</u>

- Plan every piece of work before you start writing. Don't just bumble in. You'll waste loads of time, because you haven't gotten clear about what you're doing. Take the time up front to work out the best way to complete a task. Think it all the way through.

- Be proactive. If there is a specific type of work you want to do or person you would like to work for, speak up about it!

- Don't stress – no one expects you to be an expert – they expect you to make mistakes/mess up! But when you do, don't make excuses, just figure out how to fix it.

- [On your first day in a new team] don't be

afraid to walk around and introduce yourself to everyone in your team, even if someone doesn't offer to take you around (which they should).

- There is no such thing as a stupid question. Well there is, but most of the time we think that it may be regarded as a stupid question, because we feel we ought to somehow already know the answer. Always ask. You'll waste hours working on an assumption that is probably wrong or missing some key fact, unless you ask and ensure that you understand exactly what you're being asked to do. It will make life much easier and work much more pleasurable. Remember, your supervisors were there once, too!

- There isn't a one size fits all. You don't have to be a clone of your supervisors. We are all different and operate in different ways. You can be the lawyer you want to be. You may not know what that is just yet, but remember to distinguish between being taught law and being taught personality. Soak up the former but reject the latter.

- Take a notebook wherever you go and take good notes of calls/meetings, even if not asked to.

- Don't get too excited and jump on every

piece of work you're given – speak to your supervisor about how much you should take on so you don't end up swamped/failing to deliver.

- As a trainee it's easy to get monopolised by the loudest, pushiest partner. Make sure you don't let down other members of your team just because they don't bark so loudly.

- If you are hungover at work, take a notepad with you everywhere and write everything down. You can't rely on your tired brain to catch the details. You will remember nothing without it.

- Work life balance is a worthwhile goal, but remember that this doesn't have to mean on a daily/weekly basis. Sometimes work will be the whole picture for a while (like closing a deal), but the balance will be in the weeks after when things calm down and you can leave at five PM.

- Ask your supervisor for feedback after big pieces of work or when a matter closes. This doesn't have to wait for your appraisal.

- Have fun. Your training contract can feel like an extension of university and it's OK to enjoy that aspect... but remember word spreads fast (this can be both a good thing and a bad thing, depending on what sort of reputation you have).

CLOSING STATEMENTS

I love being a lawyer. I really do. Sunday night blues are thankfully a thing of the past. Of course, sometimes it's incredibly demanding and stressful, sometimes I have to cancel social plans last minute and sometimes it's just plain boring. There have been times I've wanted to leave law altogether. Sitting at my desk at midnight, waiting for an email to come through, Googling 'how do I become a yoga instructor in Thailand' and wondering what the hell I was doing with my life. But I'm very pleased that I didn't quit.

I was so hard on myself back then. I thought I'd never, ever be good at this. The truth was I just hadn't given myself time to work things out and work out how to make them work for me and my style of practise. It takes time to learn and to consolidate that learning. You aren't a total dolt; this is hard.

It's hard, and it's worth working for. What I didn't expect to find was my passion for the law growing alongside my skill at being a lawyer. Passion truly does come from mastering a skill which earns you recognition and rewards.[42] The better you get at something the more you enjoy doing it. It's so uncomfortable when you first start out. We aren't the sort of people who are used to doing things poorly or we wouldn't be lawyers! I hope that this book has helped to speed up the learning process for you, so you can spend less time on silly mistakes and self-flagellation and more on getting stuck in and getting ahead.

We are so lucky to do (very) handsomely paid work that is intellectually stimulating, in refined offices, alongside other brilliant people. We don't 'have to' stay late to do a good job, or work at the weekend to improve our subject knowledge, we 'get to' do so. It's a privilege to do what we do. There are dues to be paid, late nights to be had, but in the long run we are winning at life. I'm so excited for us. After all, we are just getting started!

Stay hungry. Stay kind.

Katherine

---

[42] See Cal Newport's work on passion: http://calnewport.com/blog/2009/11/24/are-passions-serendipitously-discovered-or-painstakingly-constructed/ and 'So Good They Can't Ignore You: Why Skills Trump Passion in the Quest for Work You Love', Cal Newport

ABOUT THE AUTHOR

I am an associate in Constantine Cannon LLP's antitrust practice in London. A UK qualified solicitor, I trained at a major London City firm, Berwin Leighton Paisner LLP, prior to joining Baker McKenzie, Brussels.

My practice focuses on EU and UK competition law, with an interest in payment services and financial regulation. I advise on a wide range of issues, including cartel investigations, horizontal and vertical agreements, and compliance matters.

Outside of the office, I can be found covered in mud at a Spartan race, lifting heavy things at the gym, or hands in the air watching my favourite bands rock out.

Find out more and get in touch with me at www.successfulsolicitor.co.uk.

Lightning Source UK Ltd.
Milton Keynes UK
UKHW02f1827060818
326846UK00027B/1434/P